STRATEGIC
PLANNING
IN
EMERGING
COMPANIES

STRATEGIC PLANNING IN EMERGING COMPANIES

STEVEN C. BRANDT
Stanford University Graduate School of Business

▲▼ **ADDISON-WESLEY PUBLISHING COMPANY**
Reading, Massachusetts • Menlo Park, California • New York
Don Mills, Ontario • Wokingham, England • Amsterdam
Bonn • Sydney • Singapore • Tokyo • Madrid • San Juan

Library of Congress Cataloging in Publication Data

Brandt, Steven C.
    Strategic planning in emerging companies.

    1. Corporate planning.   I.   Title.
HD30.28.B7   658.4′012   80-25953
ISBN 0-201-00942-0

Eleventh Printing, July 1989

ISBN 0-201-00942-0
KLMNOPQRST-HA-89

For my wife, Wooly,
and our sons, Eric and Peter.

Contents

SECTION ONE: PERSPECTIVES 1

    1. **Dimensions of Strategic Planning 3**

    2. **Managing by Objectives 11**

    3. **How Businesses Grow 18**

    4. **Summary on Perspectives 26**

SECTION TWO: PLANNING 29

    5. **Selecting Planning Units 31**

    6. **Hierarchy of Planning Techniques 35**

    7. **The Planning Process 53**

    8. **Summary on Planning 61**

SECTION THREE: BEYOND PLANNING 63

    9. The Search for Competitive Advantages 65

   10. Cultivating a Corporate Culture 70

   11. Managing versus Doing 77

   12. Strategic Management in Emerging
      Companies 86

READINGS 95

    I. Evolution and Revolution as Organizations Grow 97

   II. Creativity by the Numbers 111

  III. Norton Company 124

  IV. Putting Excellence into Management 156

   V. Corporate Culture: The Hard-To-Change Values that
     Spell Success or Failure 164

  VI. Type Z Organization: A Corporate Alternative to
     Village Life 175

Preface

This book is written to be used. Sound strategies are usually simple. Simple strategies come from straightforward thinking by informed executives and managers. The contents of this book reflect my attempt to pull together the best from the real world of actual practice and from academia in a coherent, readable fashion. The book is organized into three sections, Perspectives, Planning, and Beyond Planning for easy reference.

Perspectives, the first section, deals with the reasons top people in fast-growing companies have to change some of their managing practices as their companies prosper. Without a developed point of view on what emerging companies are up against as they ascend into the limelight, time for the more abstract matter of positioning the company beyond the current budget cycle will be hard to justify. It's easy to get excited about strategic matters these days, given all the hullabaloo in the form of seminars, books, and consulting services. But more often than not the excitement evaporates in the heat of day-to-day pressures once the affected manager returns from his or her reverie to the firing line. The only antidote to this tendency—and it seems to be particularly acute in entrepreneurs—is information on what it takes to "keep on succeeding" in an increasingly complicated world. With $50 million in sales, a manufacturing company used to (1955) qualify for the bottom rung of the Fortune 500 ladder. Not any more. Just working hard and hoping used to go a long way toward building a company. Not any more. Identifying corporate objectives, strategies, and values—even by other names—used to be mostly a matter of extrapolating the past; such an approach seems unlikely to produce blue ribbons in the 1980s and 1990s. Perspectives on the changing times is prelude to planning for them.

Planning, the second section of this book, could have been subtitled The Mysteries of Strategic Planning Unveiled. The flood of material and experts on strategy matters in recent years has tended to obscure the basics and intimidate the successful growth company manager who senses he or she needs to do some things differently, but who has been unable or unwilling to go back to school, hire a consultant, or add a staff expert to find out what is new. In the second section we will cover planning units, techniques, and processes with a bias toward action—trying things out and keeping what works.

The final section, Beyond Planning, assumes that by then you, the reader, are nodding your head yes and are anxious to get on with putting the ideas about strategic planning in emerging companies to work in your particular corporate culture. Beyond Planning attempts to round out the picture and reduce the chance of false starts. Strategic planning is not the whole story of what top managers do—particularly in emerging companies that, by definition, are still in a highly formative state. Executives in such companies must be alert to opportunities, the kinds of opportunities—an unexpected joint venture offer, a research breakthrough, a surprise in the level of government spending, etc.—that cannot be planned. What proper, longer-range planning can do, however, is to place the enterprise in or near one or more appropriate opportunity streams so the probability of good things happening to it increases.

The top team of an emerging company can be likened to the skipper and crew of a racing yacht entered in a transoceanic contest such as the Transpac or Bermuda races. An intended course is plotted from the starting line on the mainland to the destination (Hawaii or Bermuda). That initial course is selected to take into account the "environmental factors," such as the anticipated location of the famous Gulf Stream or the perennial Pacific high-pressure area and the forecasted weather; the course chosen also takes into consideration the competition, talents of the crew, and capability of the vessel—the classic "policy" considerations for any enterprise. But once underway, the basic course is subject to confirmation or revision as new information on actual conditions is accumulated. There's no quarrel with taking advantage of a favorable wind shift or bearing off to avoid a storm. The test is to reach the objective intact and ahead of competition, given the conditions encountered. The winning skippers usually have a well-reasoned initial course (strategy) and the discipline to systematically update it in an effort to remain continually in the most favorable circumstances for victory.

There is one technical flaw in this analogy, however. Barring disaster, a racing yacht reaches its objectives sooner or later; for an emerging company, the objectives keep receding into the distance like the horizon. So, in a sense, the executive team's work is never done. That is what gives strategic planning in an emerging company its special flavor. It's a matter of plotting a course to "keep on succeeding," indefinitely. And the magnitude of the task is what makes a serious planning activity hard to begin, ticklish to synthesize, murder to implement, and overall, quite time consuming if done effectively. But the payoff can be big—to the individuals involved and society at large. It's hard to quit doing what made you successful in the past. Yet for executives who have their enterprises on the move in that gap between the survival stage and being a heavy-weight competitor, there is little choice. The complexities of the times require the processing of a lot of information, a view beyond the current budget cycle, and a systematic sorting of the products, services, and markets of the business to decide where to invest and divest a limited number of key people and dollars. That's what strategic planning is all about. It involves both questions of what we will become and how we will become it.

Much of what is in this book comes from my exposure to people like Dick Lee at Siliconix; Bert Bowers, Paul Freiman, and Bill Gomez at Syntex; Odette Ueltschi at Swiss Bernina; and Willy Pfister at Bahlsen International. These officers and thousands like them are building the leading companies of tomorrow. This book is written to serve them as a sign post along the way.

Palo Alto, California   S.C.B.
October 1980

SECTION ONE
PERSPECTIVES

Dimensions of Strategic Planning 1

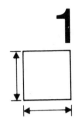

"Chance favors the prepared mind."

Louis Pasteur

The language of management is very imprecise. Words like objectives, strategy, and policy generally have meanings that vary between companies and even between individuals within companies. One useful by-product of an effective strategic planning process in a rapidly growing organization is that it can facilitate communication between members of the management team by forcing them to agree upon and use a vocabulary.

> **P: Members of strong competitive teams speak a common language of action.**

This perspective applies to the shared experience of this book, too, where the reader and the writer are joining together to examine a line of thinking competitive with past practices as well as other points of view about how to grow a business in the last two decades of the twentieth century. Here are the definitions of the critical words in this chapter.

Objective: End result to be accomplished. Typically stated in measurable terms with a targeted completion date.

Strategy: Summary statement of how objective(s) will be pursued. Note: *Strategy* planning is a subactivity of *strategic* planning.)

Structure: System of formal human relationships established to carry out plans.

Policy: Standing decision made in advance about a repetitive matter of significance to the conduct of the enterprise. (Note: The terms *"policy* making" and "business *policy"* have historically referred to aspects of a senior manager's job that are broader than standing decisions. Such broader aspects are today frequently called strategic planning.)

Planning: Predetermining a course of action to which resources will be committed. In a business setting, *strategic* planning deals with market-positioning issues and directions beyond the current budgeting cycle.

Two or more of the first four terms identify the questions that managers at different organizational levels seek to answer as they begin a planning assignment. There are essentially three major levels of planning effort within the modern corporation. Each has its own primary participants, basic time horizons, and tasks—all of which become intermingled if not entangled in a fast growing company where most key people wear several hats. The table below, Levels of Planning, summarizes the range of jobs to be done.

At the corporate level, the issues that the officers and, perhaps, the board must address are suggested in the diagram. The Strategic Questions, on the top of the next page.

The answers to these questions at the corporate level provide the framework for operational planning at the business and functional levels.

LEVELS OF PLANNING

LEVELS	PRIMARY PARTICIPANTS	BASIC TIME HORIZON	DIMENSIONS	PLANNING LABEL
CORPORATE PLANNING	Senior officers	Beyond operating budget cycle	Objectives Strategy Structure Policies	Strategic
BUSINESS PLANNING	Profit center Managers	Operating budget cycle	Objectives Strategy Structure	Strategic/ Operational
FUNCTIONAL PLANNING	Department heads	Budgeted program requirements	Objectives Strategy	Operational

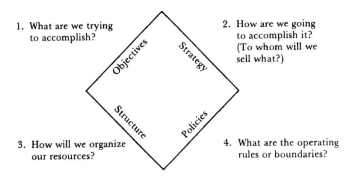

1. What are we trying
   to accomplish?

2. How are we going
   to accomplish it?
   (To whom will we
   sell what?)

3. How will we organize
   our resources?

4. What are the operating
   rules or boundaries?

THE STRATEGIC QUESTIONS

P: Officers of successful growth companies consciously separate the levels of planning.

This perspective is particularly important in the confusion accompanying rapid expansion when, for example, the distinctions between what is exciting in the profit center or the R/D department and what is good for the enterprise as a whole become muddled. The problem is compounded by the fact that the heads of the profit center and the R/D department may also be corporate officers! And the problem may be even further compounded if the company is essentially a single profit center. In such a case, the corporate and business levels of planning merge, and it is even harder for the senior people to look up from the grindstone of short-term operations and down the road ahead for the answers to the strategic questions.

Why all the fuss about levels and labels? There is a class of companies that occupy the space below the Fortune 500-size companies. Companies in this class are often characterized by managements with big ambitions and a shortage of cash, time, and staff. Yet from this class will emerge tomorrow's leaders. Some companies happen onto leadership status because of an unexpected technological breakthrough or of a windfall generated by others, such as OPEC, the government, an inept competitor, or even major customers. Other companies will successfully emerge because the top people systematically define and exploit opportunities. They cause desired things to happen. They always seem to land on their feet despite oscillations in the economy, radical swings in buying habits, and ever increasing competitive pressures caused by the success of their enterprises. How does this happen? The answer is deceptively simple. *The managers involved grow and change with the company size and complexity.* They recognize that what

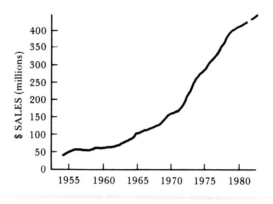

CUTOFF FOR FORTUNE 500

worked well at $50 million may not work well at $100 million. They have perspective on the changing nature of the management job.

> **P: Effective executives increase the proportion of energy devoted to planning as their enterprises expand.**

Take a look at the diagram above, Cutoff for Fortune 500. It shows what has been required to be included in the Fortune 500 over the past thirty years—the working lifetime of many readers of this book. In 1955, a company with $50 million in sales was *in* the Fortune 500. A full-fledged member!

The management of the number 500 company in the mid-1950s had $50 million worth of complexity to manage *and* a strong competitive position, perhaps even the dominant one in its industry. In the 1980s, the management of a company at even $200 million in sales has $200 million worth of complexity (people, products, markets, and so on) to manage, plus a healthy new portion of government and society to consider; and it is also *unlikely* to be a dominant competitor—for customers, talent, financing, or anything else. The "name of the game" has changed. Today relative size alone puts a premium on smartness for managements that want to move their companies up through the pack. To paraphrase a famous Peter Drucker quotation,

> *Management must increasingly be both effective and efficient. Effective means it does the right things; efficient means it does things right.*

Strategic planning is an important ingredient of effectiveness—doing the right things.

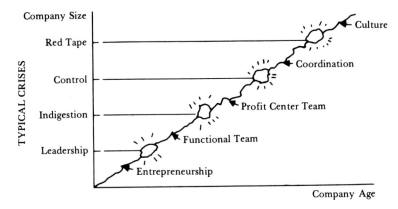

TYPICAL STAGES OF GROWTH

There's another element of perspective basic to the line of thinking expressed in this book. Over the last ten years, several scholars have analyzed various companies in an effort to discern any distinct and recurring patterns or stages of growth through which companies typically pass. Most notable among the studies was a comprehensive one done by Professor Larry E. Greiner at USC. An article describing his findings is included as Reading I in the back of this book. Overall, the conclusion reached by the researchers is that, indeed, there are some common stages and crisis points, and that an appreciation of them can assist top managers in piloting their enterprises through time. The most important stages in the corporate metamorphosis are illustrated in the diagram above, Typical Stages of Growth.*

As companies become older (x-axis) and larger (y-axis), they usually also become more complex because of either product line or market expansion, or both. More on this in Chapter 3. As a given company becomes more complex, the managing practices used by the key people need to change; often the structure of the company has to change as well. Stage one in the diagram, growth through entrepreneurship, is a well-known phenomenon. One person or a small group works long, hard, informally, and quickly to launch a new enterprise. A certain percentage of the start-ups succeed because of the energy (sweat equity) applied, but the single-minded dedication of the early executives often also contains the seeds for the first crisis: the crisis of leadership. The entrepreneur tries to do everything him- or herself; he or she

---

*Adapted from article by Larry E. Greiner, "Evolution and Revolution as Organizations Grow," *Harvard Business Review*,July-August 1972, p. 41.

won't let go of some of the reins; the company's needs exceed the grasp of the one or two individuals in the driver's seat; the enterprise bumps off the road to success.

What does it take to stay on the upward growth curve, to continue succeeding beyond what is typically the first crisis point? Usually it takes a broadening of the management talent base, some effective staffing that will become the well-rounded functional team needed for stage two growth. Such a team might include accounting or manufacturing or marketing experts depending on the needs of the business and the voids in the entrepreneur's expertise. In this second stage the entrepreneur, if he or she is to make the transition personally, must begin getting results through others, as opposed to through his or her own individual efforts. Many entrepreneurs find this a tough transition to make, and many don't make it.

In companies where the leadership hurdle is cleared, progress up the growth curve continues, products and markets are, typically, added, the business prospers and also becomes rapidly more complex. The stage is set for the second major crisis, indigestion. The single level of general management normally found in a functional organization gets to the point where it simply can no longer efficiently handle the increasingly diverse issues, problems, and questions flooding in from the various functional VPs. There is a general management overload. Schedules start being missed. Budgets get overrun. Communications bog down. Silly mistakes are made. And the quality of decisions at the top falls because the distance between the general management and the realities at the customer base has become too great. The enterprise is suffering from success. Usually the best medicine is to break the company into smaller, more manageable pieces—to decentralize into profit centers.

Stage three growth, with its multiple profit centers, means that at least one additional layer of general management has been added to the organization. This suggests that key decisions are once again made closer to the customer base, and that there is a more homogeneous character to the range of issues with which each profit center general manager must deal, since profit centers are typically formed around a single product line, piece of geography, or type of customer. Stage three growth, however, like the others, carries with it the seeds of the next crisis. The actions of independent profit centers breed the crisis of control.

Profit center managers have a tendency to go off each in his or her own direction. The total enterprise, at best, becomes merely the sum of the parts, instead of more than the sum. Corporate management gets increasingly uneasy as it senses that it's losing touch with what is going on. The direction of the enterprise becomes unclear as it stretches in various directions. Overall, things get out of control. Coordination is needed in order to exploit competitive advantages systematically—on a company wide basis. Such coordination, stage four of growth, usually takes the form of added management information systems, reporting mechanisms, and a more rigorous planning and performance review schedule throughout the year. In short, more meeting, manuals, and memos.

These moves, in time, do bring about a higher degree of coordination; experience indicates that they also can usher in the next crisis, red tape. The busy business builders in the emerging company find they are spending two-thirds of their time justifying what they do during the remaining third. The control systems developed for the decentralized company become anchors instead of sails. How is the red tape cut, or thinned, without letting the pieces of the enterprise come apart? A variety of human overrides to control systems have been tried. Examples include task forces, matrix structures, and administrative maneuvers to promote the productive interaction of seasoned people for the good of the whole organization. These overrides are sometimes successful, but not particularly enduring. A new slant on how to accomplish optimal coordination in companies with increasingly diverse activities (products/services/markets/technologies) is that the necessary control and value systems need to be *internalized* across the organization in at least the key players. Such internalization suggests the development of a corporate culture—a term that will show up with increasing frequency in management literature. The word culture implies that a group of people share a point of view about matters important to a larger enterprise of which they are a part. More on this fifth stage of growth, via corporate culture, in Chapter 10.

In summary, there are three important dimensions of strategic planning that the perceptive management team of an emerging company can use for calibration as it addresses the issues of what it is they want their enterprise to become and how they will pursue that vision. These dimensions are illustrated in the diagram, Dimensions of Strategic Planning, on p. 10.

With an awareness of the different levels of planning, the primary questions, and the historical stages of growth through which most successful companies pass, the issue of how to keep on succeeding can systematically be addressed.

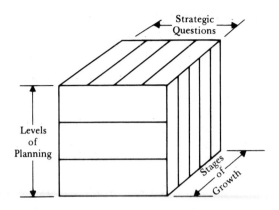

DIMENSIONS OF STRATEGIC PLANNING

Managing by Objectives

2

"Far better it is to dare mighty things . . . "
Teddy Roosevelt

With the possible exception of human relations, no management practice has received more publicity than managing by objectives (MBO). Since the concept was introduced into the corporate lexicon in the early 1960s, books, seminars, and programs on the subject have proliferated, and this has been mostly to the good. Managements around the world have picked up and legitimatized the concept during a turbulent twenty-year period when deciding with some precision what was to be accomplished, and by when, has become increasingly important. There are some horror stories, of course. And there is always the poignant question of management by *whose* objectives, employees', stock holders', or society's. But by and large, managements that select targets for themselves and their organizations are more likely to hit them than managements that operate without targets. An on-going review of how the managements of leading companies manage leads inescapably to the conclusion that an accurate perspective on this matter is

P: Individuals respond to structured expectations.

The use of objectives as a framework for managing a company is, in essence, an attempt to structure expectations. Consider the alternatives to MBO.

MANAGING BY EXTRAPOLATION (MBE)

Users of this system keep on doing what they have always done. More is normally merrier, and over time, all lines on the planning chart move upward and to the right. This essentially historical approach was adequate during the first half of this century because of the latent demand for products and services as the population in the U.S. grew in size and nature from a largely rural society to an almost completely urban one. Car companies and their suppliers produced and distributed cars; radio companies made radios; banks handled money; and so forth. Even after World War II, business was in a relatively steady state in which tomorrow could be reasonably expected to look a lot like yesterday, and the primary task for top managers was to do the same things right—that is, more efficiently. A look at the national productivity curve during this period shows that, in total, business managements succeeded in doing things right.

MANAGING BY CRISIS (MBC)

This system, long the specialty of the entrepreneur, has picked up a larger following in recent times for two reasons. First, business life as outlined in Chapter 1, is much more complex than it used to be. So there are more crises to be handled—enough, in fact, to occupy everyone pretty much full time, if they are willing. Second, there are a great many more engineers in positions of management responsibility today, and as a group they tend to be great problem solvers. Give them a crisis and they will smother it with energy and innovation. And if there should be a gap in the flow of problems, chances are good that one can be invented—something nice and tangible a manager can get his or her arms around—or teeth into. Management by crisis is popular; at the end of any given day, no one can say the boss didn't earn his pay.

MANAGING BY SUBJECTIVES (MBS)

As the cat said to Alice as she hesitated along the path to Wonderland, if you don't know where you are going, any road will take you there. There are companies that operate successfully this way. Everyone does the best he or she can to accomplish what he or she thinks should be done. Somewhere up in the organization there is presumed to be a guiding star. And there could well be. As long as the business lends itself to master minding (or central processing) by a single individual or a small team, implementation is relatively straightforward, and not much talent is needed below the top level. The mystery approach to managing has been and is a viable alternative. However, for an emerging company, the days are numbered for such an approach to managing.

One of the prices of rising from obscurity to visibility is that the dynamic company becomes the object of attention—by Naderites and government agencies and stockholders and analysts and the press. Who is the company hiring? Who is it trying to hire? Who is it firing? Why? Where is it headed? What are the projections? How big is the market share? What is the trend? And so on. "No comment" is an unacceptable answer. A dictionary definition of the word "subjective" is

> . . . *existing or originating within the observer's mind or sense organs and, hence, incapable of being checked externally or being verified by other persons.*

A subjective approach to employees' concerned questions—Where are we headed? How are we doing? How am *I* doing?—is unlikely to attract and hold the caliber of people required to capitalize on a competitive advantage. Few enterprises do more than one thing really well. The presence of a continuing and overriding business value can serve as a rallying point—if people know what it is.

MANAGING BY HOPE (MBH)

Most readers over forty years old recognize that the pace of living in the corporate world has increased markedly in recent years. Every business decision—staffing, capital investment, new services, etc.—has more ramifications than before. Certainties are hard to find. And the uncertainties of the times have led some managements into willy-nilly diversification in the hope that going in all directions at once will work out, and other managements into paralysis by analysis while they hope something will turn up to point the way for the enterprise. MBH is, essentially, a form of reacting, rather than acting, of letting events control management rather than vice versa. It is the other end of the spectrum from MBO.

Establishing measurable, dated objectives in the major areas in which results are clearly needed is a step necessary to useful strategy formulation. In the absence of objectives, any road, or strategy, will take you there. For example, one of the major new electronics companies in California's Silicon Valley has an explicit corporate objective to maintain a steady level of employment for its employees. The existence of that objective alongside the more traditional ones concerning financial performance most assuredly has had and will continue to have an impact on decisions concerning new products, plant locations, and promotion policies. Hewlett Packard, another company that has successfully emerged over the past twenty years, has historically had a corporate objective to grow at a rate consistent with the availability of internally-generated

CORPORATE OBJECTIVES

funds. This objective has influenced dividend policies, R/D direction, and marketing strategies. In short, a strong case can be made for investing whatever management time it takes to hammer out and get agreement on the objectives of the enterprise.

Corporate objectives can usefully be classified in three categories shown above in the diagram above, Corporate Objectives.

Financial Performance

Under this heading are the traditional operating-statement measures, such as sales growth and profitability. There is a strong movement today to place more emphasis on return on investment (ROI) and other balance sheet factors. The feeling properly is that in these inflationary times, single-factor measurements like sales don't give an accurate picture of how the organization is performing.

Market Performance

In this category there are a young set of measures pertaining to relative position in the market place, new produce revenues, and other innovation indicators. Interest in market performance was stimulated in the 1970s in the wake of the popularization of experience curves and market-share phenomenon. More on this in chapter 5.

The Five Es

This is the toughest category for several reasons. It is a new category to the corporate world in general, so there is a lot of confusion and consternation about how to handle it. It is also new, of course, to emerging companies not long from the survival stage where "citizenship" issues were, and to an extent still are, dead last on the list of things to worry about. And finally, performance against objectives on such matters as employment, environment, ethics, equality, and energy—the five Es—is often difficult to measure and awkward to report. Results frequently require dehumanizing body counts or complex explanations that do not lend themselves to abbreviated media coverage; and they are, therefore, hard to get across in a convincing fashion to the concerned constituency, whether it is the Sierra Club, a Congressional ethics committee, or whatever.

Who in an emerging company needs to be involved in the objectives of the enterprise, the identity and location of the goal lines? There is increasing evidence that both boards of directors and employees do—the people on each side of the management. Where a company is heading is no longer solely the prerogative of the top management. Nor does it need to be. The company that excels between now and the year 2000 will be the one that can attract and hold talented, motivated people at all levels, including the board. Such people have alternatives—other places to live, work, and develop social roots and networks. It is unlikely that an emerging enterprise can successfully extend its track record without seriously including the cultivation of its human resources as one of the results to be achieved. Regular boss-subordinate interchange on setting objectives and evaluating performance in accomplishing them can provide the central nervous system for the high-growth company. The systematic use of objectives may well be the single most important management practice for keeping a company together and on track. Objectives are the structured expectations.

Bob Noyce, cofounder and Vice-Chairman of Intel, put the issue this way*:

> *I think there's a lot of lip service given to MBO, and it's not practiced. But here everybody writes down what they are going to do and reviews how they did it, how they did against those objectives, not to management, but to the peer group and management. So that's also a communication mechanism between various groups, various divisions, et cetera.*

*Robert N. Noyce, "Creativity by the Numbers," *Harvard Business Review*, May-June 1980, p. 123.

Intel's revenues have increased each year from 1976 to 1978 by 43% compounded; its profit margin is over 20%, twice that of the rest of the industry; the company will have a billion in sales in the early eighties. The complete article describing Noyce's point of view is included as Reading II in the back of this book.

Given this perspective, how does a willing executive proceed? Objective formulation should be the kickoff point for a strategic planning process. This sequencing does not preclude iteration at later steps. A company in Chicago decided it wished to sustain a compound growth rate of 36% over its arbitrary planning period of the coming three years. Subsequent analysis and due consideration of alternative strategies for meeting that ambitious figure revealed that the figure simply could not be met without a major acquisition effort. A decision was reached to lower the objective to a more conservative 25%, a level at which the company could continue concentrating on what its management felt it could do best.

Financial performance objectives are relatively easy compared to those concerning market positioning matters and the five Es. A company's industry, competitors, dedicated stock market analysts, and bankers all provide handy reference points that help identify appropriate standards. The top management of Boise Cascade directed a dramatic turnaround in the company's fortunes after the company nearly went under in 1972. Near the start of the comeback, a decision was reached that the primary financial indicator of success would henceforth be the return on equity (ROE) of Boise as compared to the ROE of a set of major competitors in the forest products industry. ROE was chosen, according to Cliff Morton, the Vice-President of Corporate Planning, "in order to put management on the same footing as the stockholders." The strategic planning process and the management incentive system were keyed to the ROE criterion. In 1972 Boise Cascade's ROE was 3.5%; its selected set of competitors averaged 10.1%. In 1976 Boise achieved 10.7%; its competitors averaged 14.9%. In 1979 Boise reached 15.7%; its competitors averaged 16.5%—the gap nearly eliminated. During the same period Boise's stock price rose from $8 to $35, reflecting the vastly improved financial performance of the company.

Market performance, particularly market share, has come into vogue under the stimulus of various consulting companies, which center their work on the experience-curve phenomenon, and the Strategic Planning Institute, which has publicized profit impact of market strategies (PIMS) studies showing a high correlation between market share and ROI. "If you can't be number one or number two in a specific market, you had best consider getting out," paraphrases a *Wall Street*

Journal front page article describing the movement toward a market-share view of the world. Some of the evidence favoring market share is compelling, but just how the market is defined is a very significant detail. Since most emerging companies do not occupy the driver's seat *vis-a-vis* their competition, selecting market-performance objectives must be done with some care, including a healthy dose of realism. More on market-share matters in Chapter 6.

The five Es, the third major category of corporate objectives is the hardest to nail down—or to take seriously in an emerging company. "Let the big boys worry about such things," is often the attitude. But the facts are that employment, environment, ethics, equality, and energy are here to stay. The company that addresses the subjects sooner will be ahead of those that address it later or under duress. Corporate intentions and activities in these areas must be escalated to, at least, a nearly equal footing with financial and, lately, market concerns. Examples are showing up that managements are beginning to accept degrees of responsibility for objectives in the areas of employment stability and job creation, waste treatment, worldwide ethical conduct, a work force representative of the population mix, and energy conservation. These issues are slowly coming to roost at the only home where roosting is actually possible—in the business enterprises that will set the pace in the decades ahead. Neither government, unions, universities, nor foundations have the capability to respond meaningfully to the requirements of the times. Corporate objectives in the five E's will be a fact of life in the upcoming generation of companies that will challenge and/or take their places in league with companies such as Procter & Gamble, 3M, IBM, and McDonald's—companies generally considered "well-managed."

In brief, managing *with* objectives implies selecting and making the right things happen in a busy, shrinking world.

How Businesses Grow 3

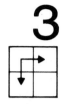

> We work day after day, not to finish things, but
> to make the future better . . . because we will
> spend the rest of our lives there.
> *Charles F. Kettering*

The typical progression of a successful growth business from its inception through various stages of growth was covered in Chapter 1. Such a business—whether it be an independent enterprise or a division of a large corporation—is normally piloted in the earlier stages by ambitious souls who work long and late to fill the cash and people voids caused by either the sudden excess or continuing lack of orders. In football parlance, quarterbacks spend most of their time scrambling in pursuit of the next first down (often a purchase order) to keep a drive down the field going.

This chapter does not cover scrambling techniques; rather it focuses on the management issues of companies that have passed beyond the problems of month-to-month existence and meeting the next payroll. Such problems are intellectually simple compared to those that confront the senior people of an enterprise—or, again, company or division—that has come into its industry's big leagues as a viable competitor. Such an enterprise has a number of opportunities before it, limited resources, of course, and a host of new factors with which to contend. Because the enterprise is no longer just another struggling small business out of view of the major players—the industry leaders, unions, government agencies, corporate neighbors that wish to pirate able people, and so on—the president can no longer make the needed first downs by merely charging repeatedly into the line. The moment comes when the contents of the *Harvard Business Review* and the nonfinancial coverage of the *Wall Street Journal* suddenly seem as though they might have some applicability to the company. But, of course, there is no time to read them. The joys of being small and quick on the feet are behind, and the benefits of being part of the establishment are still in the distance. The day finally arrives when the notion that we need a "long-term strategy" enters the discussions between the key players in a whisper. Strategy gradually becomes a nonacademic consideration in management's concerns about the best ways to build the business in the days ahead.

An early reaction to thinking beyond the current operating cycle is that the range of alternatives for building the business is infinite. *Strategic* strategy planning often appears as a giant mysterious process requiring some wizardry. This view is false. The basic strategies for building a business are finite and proven; they are six in number. They all revolve around the fundamental question of to whom are you selling what, the *sine qua non* of capitalism. They are depicted in the diagram, Basic Strategies for Building a Business.

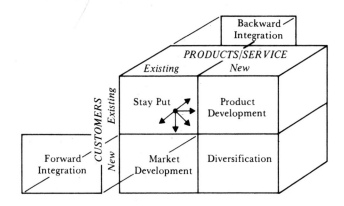

BASIC STRATEGIES FOR BUILDING A BUSINESS

Each of the six basic strategies, Stay Put, Product Development, Market Development, Forward Integration, Backward Integration, and Diversification, require certain specific skills to be executed successfully over time.

P: More people can understand a simply strategy.

Stay Put

The starting point for building the company of tomorrow is what the enterprise is doing now. Existing products and/or services are being sold to an existing set or type of customers. An upstate New

York winery is selling its bottled output to supermarkets; a $100 million Phoenix consulting firm is selling contract research to the DOE, DOD, and DOT; and a Palo Alto pharmaceutical company is selling ethical drugs to pharmacy wholesalers and promoting the products through physicians in certain selected medical specialties. When does it make sense to attempt to move off the Stay-Put corner, to alter or extend the corporate or business strategy? A management team should generate plans to extend its strategy beyond staying put when systematic analysis indicates that the enterprise can no longer meet its objectives there. Business periodicals clearly document an endless trail of companies that stopped succeeding because the demand for what they did is no more—the buggy whip syndrome. The signal that a major change in strategy may be called for is illustrated in the diagram below, Comparing Forecasts to Objectives.

Point A represents the starting point—how the company is performing and positioned now. Point B represents the projections of how the company will be performing at the edge of the planning horizon, typically two to five years ahead if current activities are continued. Point C represents the locus of corporate objectives at the edge of the planning horizon—where and what management would like the enterprise to be. If points B and C are not reasonably close together, a change in strategy may be the way to close the gap.

Consider the requirements of a sound decision to change strategy away from Stay Put. (Incidentally, staying put *includes* product-line extensions and market expansion at the margin, for instance in small increments closely related to existing activities.) First, management members must know to whom they are selling what, now. Second, they have to have projections in which they have confidence about what is likely to happen between now and the edge of the planning horizon. And third, they must have a reasonably clear picture of what the enterprise

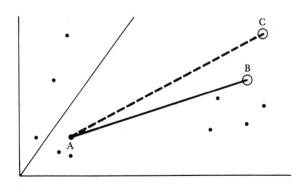

COMPARING FORECASTS TO OBJECTIVES

is out to accomplish, what its objectives are. When there is a gap between the desired and the projected results, either a change in strategy or a change in objectives may be warranted.

Consider this example. The executives of a very successful specialty chemical company in the southeastern U.S. came to the conclusion that to continue their exciting sales growth, overseas expansion and major new equity money would be required. They felt that such moves would drastically alter their life styles as scientist-managers, and they decided to alter their sales growth objectives in favor of other objectives that better reflected their professional and personal preferences. The board agreed with the alterations. No change in strategy was initiated.

Suppose a change in strategy is warranted. Product development and market development are the traditional means to grow a business.

Product Development

Many startups during the last ten to twenty years have been based on black boxes or other single-product concepts. The new idea—a failsafe electronic instrument, metal skis, a birth control pill, an insurance specialty, a resoleable athletic shoe—provides the blast off, but it seldom has sufficient power to provide sustained flight, let alone to attain higher and higher altitudes. Follow-on products to extend on the initial customer franchise become an option (or challenge) for the management. Most emerging company managements pick up the option and do, indeed, pursue a significant level of product development in building the business.

Product development, when consciously and systematically pursued as the primary strategy for building the business, requires certain talents and disciplines that are *not otherwise needed*—for example, research and/or development management. Then later, if research and development are carried out successfully, the general management team typically finds itself with a widening array of products that bring in their wake an exponentially increasing number of issues concerning market introductions, pricing, inventories, and the investment of even more R/D dollars. These issues frequently cascade into a new layer of pressure on the decision makers, a layer that can become quite annoying if the commitment to the strategy is faint-hearted.

Market Development

Geographic expansion is as old as the country: start locally; expand regionally; go national. The fast-food chains have followed this formula in recent times, as well as service companies like banks, accounting firms, and several of the major executive-recruiting organizations. Overseas expansion has become commonplace for both domestic fast-growth companies that are going abroad and foreign companies investing in the U.S. The Bahlsen company of Hanover, Germany has, for example, recently opened a pilot group of retail cookie and bakery specialty stores in the U.S. to test the chocolate-chip cookie boom in new, enclosed shopping malls. One of the largest insurance companies in the U.S. has just recently completed and committed itself to a strategic plan based almost completely on opportunities around the Pacific.

Successful market development pursued on any significant scale as a growth strategy, like any other strategy, requires certain capabilities that are not necessarily in the inventory of the emerging company. For example, broad geographic coverage complicates decision making and dilutes management control in the absence of a comprehensive management information system. The development of new market segments—new types of customers, for example—may require managers or salespeople or delivery/pricing/inventory systems that are radically different, even though the product being sold is still essentially the same. For example, more than one electronics company has been burned when it attempted to market its industrial products to retailers.

The problems with any major change in strategy are solvable; but as a company grows through creating customers in multiple markets served through several channels of distribution, the necessary resources have to be forthcoming so the company can contend with entrenched competitors, some of which are probably larger (having more resources) and some of which are probably smaller (having a faster response time and lower overhead). This fact of life highlights the need to make strategy selection a serious and conscious matter, particularly when it involves a deviation from what has been done previously. It's most often folly to tiptoe timidly into a major market development or product development or diversification effort. It's even worse to go halfheartedly in all these direction at once, managing by hope again!

P: Commitment to a strategy should be thoughtful, long-term, and unequivocal.

Many emerging companies grow fairly large without formally thinking through just where they are heading and just what they are becoming. Many emerging companies don't graduate to the major leagues either. Frequently a cause of stopping to succeed is that both product and market-development strategies are undertaken simultaneously as shown in the diagram, Typical Multidirectional Growth Strategy on the next page.

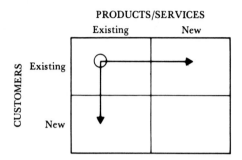

TYPICAL MULTIDIRECTIONAL GROWTH STRATEGY

With a multidirectional strategy, it is easy to imagine how the job of the general managers can quite quickly become more complicated. Often increased complexity leads to organizational constipation. Deadlines for schedules, budgets, and key events are missed, which in earlier times would have been met by dint of extra energy and time provided by the top people. Now, however, the company has become too big for such fixes except for an occasional grand-slam emergency. One of the planning tasks at the corporate level in a company is to establish boundaries on the range of alternative strategies that will be considered. For example, it is not unusual to find limits to diversification established.

Increasing complexity, also, often turns management to organizational restructuring for a solution to the new problems. By realigning the parts of a business, oftentimes the complexities can be divided and reduced to more manageable sizes. Organization design is a proper question for top management, and generally, structure should follow and support strategy.

There are three other basic growth strategies for building a business.

Forward or Backward Integration

Forward integration means that a company is moving up the distribution chain by investment and activity in order to be closer to the consumer of its products or services. Both Xerox and Texas Instruments, for example, are experimenting today with retail stores for their services and products.

Backward integration means that a company either acquires its supplier, or invests in facilities to replace those suppliers. Backward integration can be undertaken as a means of growing or of guaranteeing needed resources, or for both reasons. *Vertical integration* in either direction has been a popular strategy since the early days of industrialization when the managements of the original set of emerging companies (steel, autos, chemicals, oil, and so on) "fully integrated" their enterprises. The need to integrate for defensive reasons is probably less frequent today than it was then; board-room arguments for an integration strategy in the 1980s or 1990s will probably revolve more around value-added opportunities or the absence of other, more attractive strategy scenarios for growth.

Diversification

Except perhaps at the corporate level of planning in a holding company—that is, in a conglomerate—this last basic strategy is the most difficult to execute successfully because it generally requires a management team to move the farthest afield from its proven area of expertise. New products *and* new markets, both at the same time, suggest a big challenge. Few professional venture capitalists will invest in a deal that lacks a well-rounded management team with a proven record of success in doing what is proposed to be done in the future. Yet the graveyard of great ideas is full of ill-fated diversification moves (many born in the 1964–1974 era) by effective executives who assumed, for example, that success in medicines is transferable to cosmetics, that a can company can do well in hit records, that experience with diesel motors is great for ski manufacturing and marketing, and that condominiums are a natural adjunct to banking. Diversification is a tough strategy to execute well over time. It is the distant cousin of finding a niche and filling it. But sometimes it is necessary.

Government regulation of certain industries is forcing alert, affected managements to broaden the bases of their enterprises by diversification. The nuclear reactor business is a case in point. General Atomic has for years been a leader in a second-generation technology for nuclear power plants. But the market for all forms of nuclear power has, essentially, dried up. General Atomic had little choice from a rational business standpoint but to redirect its impressive human resources (1000 engineers and scientists) into new areas of endeavor such as contract research, consulting, and the development of other (nonnuclear) energy products.

Diversification for the *typical* emerging company, however, will most often be the court of last resort from a strategy selection standpoint.

A final introductory word of perspective on how businesses grow. As a class of people, growth-company executives and managers are a smart, hardworking, achievement-oriented bunch. But they have only the standard allocation of wizards and geniuses among them. The author has yet to meet one that didn't put his or her pants on one leg at a time. When it comes to strategy formulation, it is execution of the fundamentals that pays off. In professional football, to paraphrase Vince Lombardi, the team that runs, blocks, passes, and tackles well, consistently, is going to come out the winner. In professional managing, the team that outlines a clear picture of what it wants to become and systematically plans, supervises, and controls the use of its resources to get there, is likely to do so.

Summary On Perspective

4
P:

> "A wise man will hear and increase in understanding."
>
> *Proverbs* 1:5

The challenge for the managers of an emerging company is to continually adjust their managing practices to ones that allow their enterprise to keep on succeeding. It is safe to assume that much of what worked well yesterday will not work as well tomorrow. This is so for two distinct reasons. Corporations, in general, are the focal point of rapid social change; emerging companies compound the rate of change by growing faster than average. Increasingly effective planning that goes above and beyond the operating cycle is an important way of getting at the right questions en route to sound decisions about where to invest and divest cash and key people.

To justify or rationalize stepping back from the familiar day-to-day issues where he or she has proved him or herself in order to allocate new time to the more abstract, strategic issues of objectives, strategies, structure, and policies, a dynamic company executive requires perspective. The preceding three chapters have provided it by highlighting how much the ante to enter the Fortune 500 class of companies has increased and what the various stages of growth are through which most companies typically pass en route to maturity. In addition, the use of explicit objectives as an entry point to strategy formulation is tagged as a necessity, not an option, for an enterprise of any complexity. "In the long run, men hit only what they aim at," said Henry Thoreau. And finally, some of the mysteries that surround strategic planning, the subject of this book, were unveiled by a review of the range of basic strategies for building a business.

At the corporate level of a multibusiness company, much of the strategic planning effort is directed first at establishing boundaries for product development, market development, vertical integration, and diversification. Then, second, the officers must pick and choose where to invest and divest among the businesses in a manner that reflects both what the corporation is aiming to become and the magnitude of the resources available.

At the business level, or at the corporate level of a single-business company, the process is much the same—boundaries first, sorting and selecting among opportunities second—except that the units under discussion are different. More on that in the next chapter. At either level, corporate or business, the seven perspectives suggested in the preceding chapters apply. They are restated below in an action format to facilitate their use.

- Establish a management vocabulary within the company.
- Separate the levels of planning: corporate, business, and functional.
- Increase the proportion of executive energy devoted to planning as the enterprise expands.
- Structure expectations throughout the organization.
- Keep major strategies simple.
- Support decisions with commitments.

SECTION TWO
PLANNING

Selecting Planning Units

5

In total, strategic planning is a process of systematically sorting through a corporation or business and deciding what roles the various parts will play in the future of the enterprise. To collect and analyze data en route to decisions about where cash and talent will be invested or divested, the corporation or business has to be divided into pieces or units that can be compared. Most often, in a large mature company, the units for comparison will be the operating profit centers. The "planning units" will be the existing "business units." In an emerging company, however, there may still be only one operating profit center (the whole company), or the profit centers that do exist—plants or product lines, for example—may not be ideal for useful thinking about the future.

Consider this example. One of Silicon Valley's finest young semiconductor companies was at $70 million in sales and was growing at a rate of about 30% per year compounded. It had the following characteristics:

- Six major product lines sold throughout the world.
- Three geographic profit centers: U.S., Europe, Far East. Each had a general manager reporting to the president.
- Three functional vice-presidents (marketing, R/D, finance) reporting to the president.
- Two major processes/technologies in which it excelled.
- Four major customer groups.

How should the officers think strategically about the future? It's a tough but vital question, and this team of executives followed a fairly standard progression of learning over a four-year period. Their first pass at developing a three-year plan revolved around getting the functional vice-presidents to each develop a three-year plan. This effort was interesting, and it resulted in some large three-ring binders full of material that the executive group of seven reviewed and discussed in detail. The result was a slightly more farsighted budget for the coming year and a set of numbers for the subsequent two years. However, once the annual budget was finalized, the three-ring binders were not opened again. The management continued to build the company on all fronts: three geographies, six product lines, two technologies.

The next year, the three-year planning effort had a somewhat greater sense of urgency. It was becoming obvious to a growing number of the seven officers that some of the company's internal systems were being stretched to the breaking point. Needed management information was slow in coming; inventories were harder to control; and R/D dollar allocation meetings were becoming shouting matches. This second pass at a strategic plan was focused on the three profit-center general managers. It was their turn to peer into the dim future and prepare a three-ring binder full of information and thoughts. Once again the review and discussions by the top team was useful, and a better annual plan for the coming year was generated. Even more money was allocated for upgrading the internal systems with an eye to the $130 million sales figure now projected (extrapolated) three years out. But as the reader will have already perceived, the big questions were not being addressed. What do we want to become? Assuming that we *cannot* sell everything to everybody due to our limited resources, to *whom* do we wish to sell *what* in the future? And trade-off decisions between the various parts of the business were not being made. Why not? One reason was that the planning units were not viable and that, therefore, serious planning—predetermining a course of action to which resources would be truly committed—was very difficult.

The first year, the planning units were functions; the second year they were pieces of geography. In neither case was a "no" decision possible: The company was not about to stop a function like marketing or depart from a piece of geography like Europe and channel the released resources to other parts of the company.

The third year, after seeing the second year's set of binders gather dust from January on, the top team settled on product groups as the planning units, recognizing from the start that the groups cut across organizational lines. The planning units were not the business units. For this company, the six product groups worked as the basis of the first *real* three-year plan from which the various business (organizational) units then prepared their annual plans.

What, then, are the critieria for selecting a planning unit? Each discrete planning unit should

1. *Lend itself readily to the collection of data* about market opportunities, specific competitors, investment requirements, risks, government actions, technology trends, and other factors related to the requirements for business success (sales, profits, ROI, etc.) in the future. A more complete list of possible data points will be presented in the next chapter.
2. *Be reasonably comparable to other planning units* for decision-making purposes. Apples and oranges might be OK as planning units; apples and oil wells would probably not be—even in a highly diversified conglomerate.
3. *Facilitate implementation* once decisions are reached about the mission of the unit in the company's future. Generally speaking, the unit should have a boss; that is, the overall responsibility for the unit should be assigned or assignable to an individual.

This last point is the reason business units, usually profit centers, are typically the first choice as planning units, and it is not unusual for a company to realign its organizational structure as the result of experience gained during strategic planning. But sometimes the structure must remain responsive to pressures other than those of a planning nature. In such instances, planning units can become an overlay on the organization chart, as in the following example.

> *A research-driven, Eastern pharmaceutical company with a half billion in sales worldwide and ambitious objectives tried to get a strategic planning program going for three years using their seven regions (profit centers) around the world as the planning units. The regional setup and staffing was mandatory because each country had vastly different regulatory procedures and sensitivities. Each year, with a lot of fanfare (and expensive travel), the results of the "strategic" planning effort would come out essentially the same. The regional vice-presidents would present their ideas, and then they would be told by the senior research people from the central lab precisely which products would be researched, produced, and introduced in the various countries during the planning period. It was not until the top management made the company's therapy areas (heart disease, dermatology, etc.) the primary, long-term planning units that meaningful discussions between the researchers and the regional organizations began to take place and lead to strategic decisions that were accepted throughout the company.*

As a part of this switch in planning units, a senior officer was assigned worldwide responsibility for each therapeutic area. At that point, the planning units had become an overlay on the organization chart.

Like most higher-growth companies, this pharmaceutical company had a need to clean house periodically, to prune back the range of its products, markets, and projects so that a critical mass of resources could be marshalled and channeled into the selected few opportunities most compatible with achieving the company's established objectives. Such prunings, however, are not painless because there are seldom historical activities within a company that do not have strong advocates.

Strategic planning is a discipline that helps managers and executives examine the various parts of the enterprise with a collective and, it is hoped, an objective eye. As a result of the examination, it normally becomes apparent that different products, services, divisions, markets, technologies, or combinations of these have different capabilities (to generate cash, for example,) and different longer-term potentials. Putting selected parts together in a synergistic, coherent way is high art for the professional manager. Discrete planning units are the ingredients of alternative strategic scenarios.

Hierarchy of Planning Techniques

6

Given all the publicity on planning in recent years, it is easy to get the impression that it is something new. Yet a look at the history of entrepreneurship and enterprise in general shows that thinking ahead—in terms of what, beyond the coming year, shall be sold and to whom—is as old as business itself. To be sure, the tools and techniques of analysis have become more sophisticated, particularly in the last ten to twenty years. But that doesn't automatically make them better for or more applicable to a given company. In the same way that a professional golfer has to select his or her club for a given shot, the professional manager has to select one or more appropriate techniques to analyze and determine the relationship between his or her planning units.

In the pages that follow, a hierarchy of planning techniques will be reviewed. The hierarchy roughly parallels both time and complexity. The higher up the technique is in the hierarchy, the more recent and more costly it is to use. An important, early question to answer when going into a strategic planning process is, On what basis will we make our trade-off decisions en route to a comprehensive corporate or business strategy for pursuing our objectives?

INTUITION

35

By far the oldest and most common way of making decisions on a longer-term direction is to rely on the buried experience and judgment of the top people, those who ultimately call the shots. As Quarterback Terry Bradshaw said following his Steeler's dramatic victory in Super Bowl XIV, "Both times [before both touchdowns] that down-the-center pass play just seemed like a good thing to try. It was a new play for us; but it worked." Intuition at work. Many major opportunities in the tomorrows are not obvious; no amount of market research will ferret them out. A decision to favor one planning unit instead of another will never be based on pure science. Intuition is not obsolete; and a proper strategic planning process can hone it, as will be explored later in the Beyond Planning section of this book.

SALES VOLUME

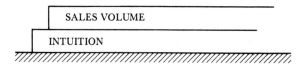

Push what's selling. Second in age and probably as common in practice as intuition are decisions made about what kinds of plants to build, which markets to enter, and where to invest research dollars—based on the relative sales volumes of the planning units, whether they are product lines, divisions, or markets. If facts about all the significant businesses in the country were put into a single data base and the right button on the computer was pushed, chances are good that the print-out would look like this:

RELATIVE
PERCENTAGE
OF RESOURCES
ALLOCATED TO
PLANNING UNIT

RELATIVE SALES VOLUME OF PLANNING UNIT

The simplicity of using sales volume as the primary sorting technique is its virtue. Its drawback, looking ahead to the year 2000, is that domestic population growth will have tapered off, technology will have caused unpredictable changes, and the value systems at all buying points will have been in continuous flux. This combination makes the premise that what is selling now will sell tomorrow increasingly suspect.

PROFITABILITY

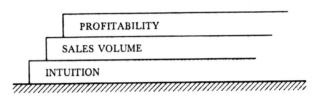

From the top line, emphasis is shifted to the bottom line. Today many major companies operate on the basis of an annual profit plan. As such managements extend their planning horizons, it is only natural that the relative profitability—expressed in either percentages or absolute dollars—of the various units be closely scrutinized.

> *In 1977, a major Midwestern company active in mining, pollution control, and fluid-handling equipment undertook a strategic planning effort separate from its traditional, annual, profit-planning cycle. The purpose was to explore a course for the eighties that would make use of the momentum built up over the previous seven years, during which time the company had grown from $70 million to $425 million in sales. The entire company was thoughtfully broken into twenty-seven planning units. The 1977 planning effort was the first time top management had looked in detail beyond the three group aggregations of mining, pollution control, and fluid handling. The senior people were surprised to find that over a third of the twenty-seven units were actually unprofitable, and almost another third were only marginally profitable. It was also news to find that of the seven units with the best projections to the planning horizon, five were the responsibility of the most conservative and least aggressive of three senior vice-presidents.*

This short example reveals one desired output that adds spice to the planning process—the strategic "ah-HAs." Such ah-HAs suddenly provide entirely new layers of insight about success and failure that years of grinding through an annual budgeting process would never reveal.

Cliff Morton, Vice-President of planning at Boise Cascade, recounts one of his management's strategic discoveries. For years the management of an important consumer-products division (a planning unit) projected the division's future on the basis of the population growth in the area the division served. A required closer look at the profitability components revealed that population growth had virtually nothing to do with the performance of the division. The real stimulus was the disposable income in the area, and that income was tied to farm prices—a very different leading indicator for the business than population.

CONTRIBUTION MARGIN

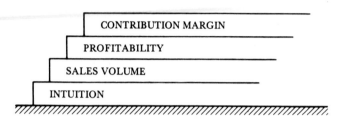

The contribution margin is a somewhat more sophisticated sorting technique than sales or profitability in that it involves a look at dollars contributed to the sum of the unallocated overhead and the absolute profits of the enterprise (contribution margin = net sales price − variable costs). This technique has a lot of applicability to younger companies that have yet to install fully developed accounting systems or that have product groups as their primary planning units. For example, a contribution margin analysis can reveal ways of increasing profits at a specified sales-volume level by simply altering the product mix sold to produce that level of sales

The three planning techniques in the hierarchy that are above intuition have so far all been single factor measures. The next step in the hierarchy is a big one.

RETURN ON INVESTMENT

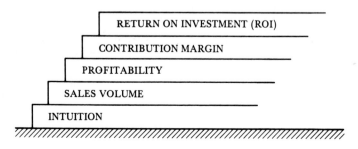

ROI analyses by planning units are quickly catching hold in growth-company management circles. With the high inflation and two recessions in the years between 1974 and 1981, managements as well as stock market devotees have become increasingly interested not only in "How well are we doing?" but also in "How much of an investment did it take to do the job?" ROI methods have been in vogue for many years for capital investment decisions; today they have broader use both in current performance measurement and strategic planning matters. ROI will increasingly become *the* basic financial performance measuring stick.

The four steps immediately above intuition in the hierarchy are all based on internally generated data. Such data are relatively easy to come by and to assimilate compared to the three steps that follow.

PRODUCT LIFE CYCLE

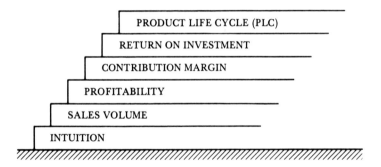

The PLC is the first sorting technique in the hierarchy, which suggests that for planning purposes what is going on outside the company in the market, industry, economy, and so on, is equal to or even more important than the records or projections based on internal data. The shape of the normal PLC curve and its major stages are shown in the following graph.

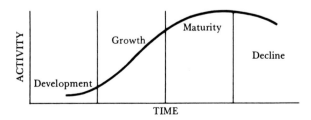

A management arraying its planning units on a PLC curve would find the ensuing discussion thought provoking. For example, suppose an enterprise had ten units and analysis indicated they all fell out like this:

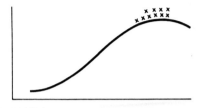

Or this:

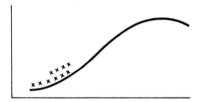

Or this:

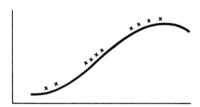

In each case, the planning implications are quite different. And, further, chances are that any PLC graph will give a significantly different picture of the business than a graph derived, for example, from an ROI analysis and projection. By nature, older established products or divisions tend to have higher and, therefore, more favorable ROI's than younger products and divisions in the same company. But the established units will also fall nearer the top of the PLC curve. Recognizing that neither long term ROI nor PLC position can be measured with even 75% accuracy, which technique, ROI or PLC, should be given preference by a given management? The answer is that probably neither should be used exclusively, but that each can be helpful to management in thinking about its business, about how the various parts of the business relate to one another, and about

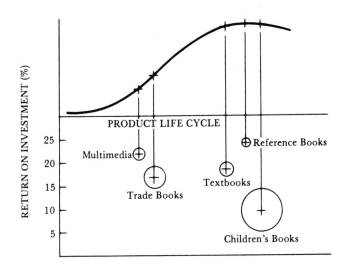

modifying those relationships to build the company of the future. It is also possible to play with combinations of the ROI and PLC techniques. For example, suppose ROI and PLC were combined on a graph and the planning units of, say, a book publishing company were plotted as shown at the top of this page.

What are the implications of this two-factor analysis to a perceptive management? Are the highest ROI units most deserving of significant additional investment? Should the Children's Book Division be injected with capital or the publisher's sharpest division manager in order to turn it around? Does the average ROI for Trade Books give it a cloudy future? Interesting issues, and a thorough airing by top management of the issues provoked by the appropriate planning technique (or techniques) is the *only* road to decisions right for the enterprise.

EXPERIENCE CURVE/MARKET SHARE

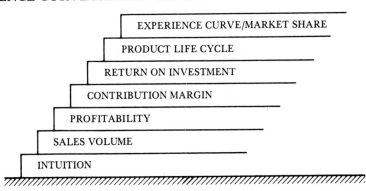

No other single planning concept has received more publicity in recent times than this modern variation on the *learning-curve* theory, which has been around since at least World War II. Underlying the theory is the notion that people doing a fairly mechanical task, over and over again, get better at it. In business terms, work hours per unit of production and, hence, labor costs per unit decrease in a predictable manner as the volume of production accumulates. Other unit costs often decrease also. In the mid-1960s, consultants breathed fresh air into this old concept to explain the cost histories of a variety of products from semiconductors to vacuum cleaners. The curve was retitled the *experience curve,* and the theory was expanded as follows:

> *Unit cost is a function of accumulated experience; that experience is a function of sales volume; and sales volume is a function of market share. Therefore, the company with the highest market share* vis-a-vis *its competitors should have relatively lower costs and, therefore, should generate more net cash. In short, cash flow is a direct function of market share, and gaining or holding a high market share relative to competitors is a strategically desirable thing to do.*

The experience-curve concept has ushered in an era of interest in market share as a critical indicator of how a planning unit is doing or possibly can do in the future. There is, of course, the problem of defining the market in which the share is measured. Almost anyone can have the dominant share of a market that is narrowly defined to match just what the definer is already doing. What is Porsche's market share? Or Apple Computer's? It depends. So, market-share consciousness— although an important new filter for straining information about a planning unit—has its limitations, particularly for emerging companies that, frequently, do not have stabilized products and markets amenable to easy definition and measurement.

Market-share analysis lends itself well to combinations with other sorting techniques in the planning hierarchy. The most well-known combination is probably the four-cell matrix popularized by one of the strategy consulting firms established in recent years. (See the matrix at the top of the next page.)

In this two-factor analysis, planning units that are Stars may be cash generators (high market share) or cash users (resulting from market growth rate). Cash Cows are former Stars whose market growth rates have declined (falling stars!) and which should generate net cash for use elsewhere in the corporation. Dogs are parts of the enterprise from which investment dollars should be extracted. Question Marks pose the issue of which of their number should be selected for investment in order for them to be moved to the left (to increase in market share) and which should be dropped (divested).

This technique is easy to understand in concept. But it is important to recognize that there are extra limitations that apply to its use in emerging companies. These limitations revolve around the difficulties in accurately defining either the relative market share or the projected market growth rates for the planning units that are often contestants in embryonic industries. For raising the quality of the thinking and discussion about strategic matters, however, this particular two-factor analysis has a great deal of merit. Consider, for example, the implications to the top managements if, following some months of intensive research by either inside or outside consultants—or by, most likely a combination of the two—the planning units of four unrelated companies fell out as follows

What follows are some possible issues suggested for useful discussion. First assume that in each of the four companies, the management feels that the data behind its matrix are *reasonably* representative of its situation; and, second, assume that the management of each company wishes to make practical use of this particular two-factor planning technique.

Company A Issues

1. Do we have enough cash to move one or more of the Question Marks to the left (to improve its market share)?
2. Can one or both of the Dogs be either moved to a stronger market position or beneficially divested?
3. Do we have internal blockages that prevent our moving attractive units into strong market positions? For example, do we have a weak marketing department?

Company B Issues

1. How big is the single Cash Cow? (Often on these four-cell charts the planning units are shown as circles with areas in proportion to the sales volumes or cash contributions of the units.)
2. How long will the Stars be shining? (What's the shape of their projected PLCs? At what point in time will the Stars become net cash generators rather than users?)
3. Do we need to consider acquisitions or to initiate an R/D effort in a search for potential future Stars?

Company C Issues

1. Is the projected performance of our combined existing planning units compatible with our corporate objectives?
2. How big is the potential of the one Question Mark, and what will it take to be number one, two, or three in the market place in terms of market share?
3. Are we lacking in innovation talent?

Company D Issues

1. Are we giving adequate attention and talent to projecting and monitoring future cash needs?

2. Is our Cash-Cow cash sufficiently large and healthy?
3. Are we developing a management pool of talent compatible with the future in which we'll have an increased number of planning units that will need to be managed for cash generation rather than growth?

These are the kinds of useful strategic issues that can be generated by a balanced planning process that systematically makes use of one or more of the available planning techniques to compare the parts of a business. Two-factor techniques stretch management thinking along more dimensions than do single-factor techniques such as those found lower in the hierarchy.

MULTIPLE-FACTOR MATRIX

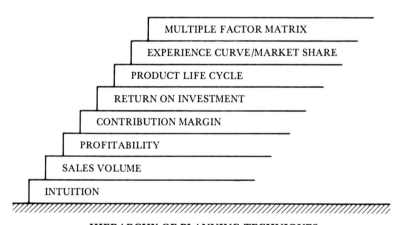

HIERARCHY OF PLANNING TECHNIQUES

At the top of the diagram entitled Hierarchy of Planning Techniques is a final technique in which the limits of single- and two-factor analyses are replaced by the complexities of trying to take into account the reality that modern managements live in a messy world. The Multiple-Factor Matrix, often dubbed the nine-cell matrix, has a horizontal axis labeled competitive position—a term broader than simply market share or PLC. It has a vertical axis labeled market attractiveness—a term broader than simply ROI or market growth rate. And the contents of these two measuring sticks is limited only by a management's imagination, time, and money.

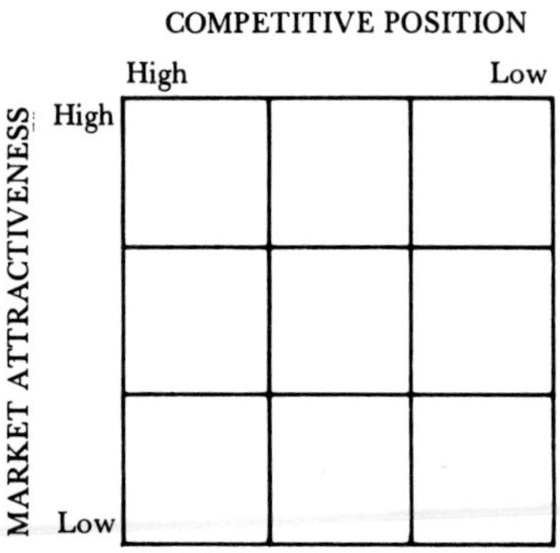

COMPETITIVE POSITION

```
                    High                    Low
           ┌─────────┬─────────┬─────────┐
      High │         │         │         │
           ├─────────┼─────────┼─────────┤
           │         │         │         │
           ├─────────┼─────────┼─────────┤
           │         │         │         │
      Low  └─────────┴─────────┴─────────┘
```

(vertical axis label: MARKET ATTRACTIVENESS)

MULTIPLE-FACTOR MATRIX

For example, the following are the components used by one medium-technology, emerging company to measure each planning unit's competitive position and market attractiveness.

COMPETITIVE POSITION

Marketing

Current Share: What is the unit's current position in relation to those of its active competitors?

Reputation with Customers: How is unit perceived and received?

Marketing Skill: Does the unit have the breadth and depth of ability to excel?

Sales Force Quality: What are the abilities of the management and salespeople?

Coverage of Market: How well does management understand the unit's customers?

Manufacturing

Value Added: What is the degree of vertical integration?

Cost Competitiveness: What is the record of improvements?

Labor Stability: Is the unit's climate and turnover generally favorable?

Control Systems: Can management predict results (shipments, costs, etc.) with confidence?

Supplies Assurance: Are key resources available?

Technical Competence

Staff Size & Quality: What is the breadth of the unit's skill base? Of its technical capability?

Record of Innovation: What is the value of its R/D results for the last three years?

New Products Introduced: What is the number of significant contributions made in the last three years?

Products

Relative Quality: What is the ranking of the unit's products compared to those of the competition?

Unique Features: What are the competitive advantages of its products including price? How comprehensive is each given line of products?

Position in PLC: What is the risk of product obsolescence or the chance of market maturity?

Planning Unit Management

Control of Business: How reliable is the management in keeping its commitments?

Competence: Does management have proven performance in all necessary functions?

Stability and Depth: Will there be managerial continuity to the planning time horizon?

Flexibility: Does the unit management anticipate and accommodate change?

Innovation/Productivity: How many fresh ideas have been developed in the past three years?

Unit Competitive Performance

Sales Growth: What is the unit's sales record as compared to plans made?

Earnings Growth: What is the unit's earnings record as compared to plans made?

ROI: How well does the unit utilize its resources?

The determination of a planning unit's competitive position requires a synthesis of two kinds of information. First, there are comparisons of the unit to competitors in the marketplace. Such comparisons may be made on the basis of hard data, "best guesses" by experienced people, or, most likely, combinations of each. Second, there are comparisons of the unit to other units within the company. For example, under the category of Planning Unit Management, an assessment is, typically, made about how the unit under consideration stacks up against the other planning units in the company. The purpose of looking at the competitive position of each planning unit in a number of ways is to identify those planning units in which the company clearly has an advantage.

Whereas the information on competitive position reflects both external and internal comparisons, the information needed about market attractiveness comes almost solely from the field. The questions determine the relative values of the markets served, or potentially served, by the various planning units.

MARKET ATTRACTIVENESS

- What are the total dollars spent by the planning unit's natural customer base?
- What is the projected rate of growth in total dollars to be spent in the future?
- In the past, what has the company earned in sales to the customer base?
- In the past, what has been the ROI on company sales to the customer base?
- How easy is it for competitors to enter into the subject market? (How high are the barriers to entry?)
- What is the cost of reaching the key buying influences in the market?
- How credit worthy are the important customers?
- How energy dependent are the important customers?
- What are the financial and marketing capabilities of the major competitors in the market?
- How much government intervention is there in the market?

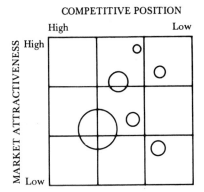

COMPETITIVE POSITION

- In the past, how quickly has the market reacted to innovations?
- How well does management know and understand the historical requirements for success in the market?

Although these two lists are not exhaustive, they worked well for one manufacturer. They *are* representative. With answers to the questions posed and points, perhaps weighted, assigned to each answer, it becomes possible to give each planning unit numerical coordinates. These coordinates can then be plotted on a multiple-factor matrix for discussion purposes. The hypothetical example at the top of this page shows six planning units plotted with circles proportional in area to sales volume.

What does a management team have when it finally gets such a matrix in front of it? Assuming that there has probably been a lengthy period of serious homework and a healthy portion of heated discussion en route to a consensus about the factors to be used and the points to be assigned to each planning unit, the management has a comprehensive, composite picture of how the various parts of the enterprise relate to one another and to the world outside. The picture isn't perfect, but it can help push the right questions to the surface. The multiple-factor matrix, just as the other techniques in the planning hierarchy, can provide management with a basis for decisions about where to allocate its resources—primarily talent and cash—in the future.

Once a management team has used a multi-factor matrix, legitimate questions are bound to arise:

1. Is the choice of planning units correct? (Did they lend themselves to data collection and analysis, and are they usefully comparable to one another?)

2. Are the data collected adequate? (Are the quality and quantity of the data sufficient for our needs?)
3. Do we believe the picture we see?
4. Now that we have this picture, what do we do with it?

There is a growing base of experience in the use of multiple-factor matrixes. Some of the early users—companies like GE—have used what is now called the Build, Hold, Harvest breakdown.

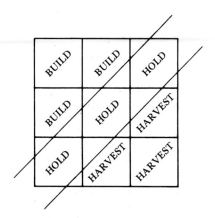

The diagonal lines between the three strategic classes are sometimes arrived at by arbitrarily dividing all the units into thirds. Other times natural divisions appear. And often no lines are used, and each of the nine cells is given a descriptive title along with possible operating implications. Overall, however, a BUILD strategic assignment means an aggressive expansion of the unit's presence in the market place. Typical operating moves to build include:

Additions to marketing and sales staffs.
Aggressive pricing.
New products.
Development of broader and stronger management talent.
Acquisitions.
Capacity expansion.

Such moves would, of course, require investment. Most likely planning units being built would have a negative short-term cash flow; they could also be a short-term drag on earnings and ROI. Such performance is acceptable, typically, if it is expected, and if it is part of an overall plan for meeting the objectives of the enterprise.

A HOLD strategic assignment suggests that the current position in the market place will be maintained *vis-a-vis* competition. Whether the market is going up or down, the planning unit will remain where it is. This type of assignment is roughly comparable with the Cash Cow of the simpler, two-factor matrix. Representative operating moves to hold a planning unit in position might include:

Careful market segmentation.

Selective product development and product-line extensions.

Vertical integration to help the company become or remain a low-cost producer.

Value engineering and productivity programs.

Tight control on working capital.

Marketing feints and tactics to confuse major competition—for instance, the preannouncement of new products.

Conservative management leadership.

Units in the HOLD class are usually those currently constituting the backbone of the business. They are, normally, strong cash earnings and ROI producers—the driving forces behind the successful emergence of the company to date.

The term HARVEST identifies the third class or strategic assignment. Harvest suggests a *controlled* loss of selective market position during which major amounts of cash are released for use elsewhere in the enterprise—usually to BUILD. In short, it means that management decides to stop doing, in a timely manner, something that it has historically done, in favor of something that is relatively more attractive. The management is looking ahead. Appropriate operating moves that might be integrated into annual plans for planning units with HARVEST assigments might include:

Raising prices.

Reducing cost-generating quality.

Allowing tooling to wear out.

Avoiding new equipment and plant investments.

Consolidating facilities.

Reducing sales, marketing, R/D, and management expenses.

Seeking buyers for parts or all of the unit.

Trimming inventories and services.

Harvesting is tough to do—first to make the decision, and second to carry it out smoothly. Most emerging-company managers are builders by nature. The Norton Company case, Reading III, in the back of the book, describes the hold-or-harvest dilemma faced by corporate and operating management when two different types of analyses produce mixed answers about what to do with a major, historical piece of the company. The Norton Company case also vividly illustrates one management team's experience in working with the techniques near the top of the Hierarchy of Planning Techniques.

The multiple-factor matrix is one of the professional manager's most complex strategic planning technique to date, because it attempts to synthesize many other techniques and judgment-calls into a single picture for management to use in sorting through its business.

The Planning Process

7

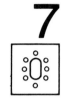

"Iron sharpens iron. So one man sharpens
another."

Proverbs 27:17

While the previous chapter provides the technical underpinning for
sorting through the parts of a business in a meaningful fashion, this
chapter is the philosophical heart of the book. In the fifteen or twenty
years that strategic planning has been rising on the management scene
as a subject worthy of attention, several lessons have become clear.
They are summarized as follows:

> *Strategic planning is a **line management activity** centered on getting
> **the right people, agenda, and information** together on **a timely sched-
> ule** in order to make **decisions that commit cash and people to market-
> place positioning assignments extending beyond the current operating
> cycle.***

LINE MANAGEMENT ACTIVITY

As suggested in an earlier chapter, the number of strategic plans in
three-ring binders that are reviewed, discussed, and then forgotten are
large. There is no implementation; there is no significant payoff. None
of the products or markets or activities of a burgeoning emerging company are pruned back so that resources can be concentrated on selected longer-term opportunities. The enterprises all grow contentedly
until ... *usually* until unexpected slowdowns in performance force
more discipline on management. How, instead, can implementation,
from the very day that planning starts, become part of the plan of what
the enterprise is to become? There is only one answer: The planners

must be the same people who will be responsible for carrying out the plan. Following are examples of three common mistakes many well-meaning executives have made.

Planning Staff

A well-known, medium-sized, consumer-products company got the strategy bug and hired a very creative, aggressive, senior executive away from a larger company in a related field to become the vice-president of corporate planning. Three years and two big strategic plans later, the executive and the position were eliminated. The consensus of the senior management was that, although the many hours spent planning had been interesting (albeit expensive), the chief planner had never really been able to come up with a comprehensive program that set well with a healthy cross section of the management.

There is a big difference between a planning director that sees his or her job as *the* architect of a company plan and one that sees it as a processor, catalyzer, or facilitator. There is a great deal of *very* important support work that an effective planner or staff can do. Think back to the planning techniques in the hierarchy covered in the previous chapter. Most require data other than that generated internally by the accounting department. The data must be generated, massaged, and put into forms useful for review and discussion. And there is plenty of opportunity for the effective planner to nudge the process in directions suggested by his or her professional expertise. However, the moment senior line managers are let off the hook and the strategic plan is identified as someone else's plan, the probability of implementation and payoff falls a long way.

Consultants

An old line northeastern company hired a major consulting firm to develop a long range plan. The consultants did a thorough job of analyzing the market, internal cost trends, and competition. The consulting team developed a comprehensive picture of the relative strengths and weaknesses of the company and accurately identified a major "gap" between where the company was likely to be in five years and where a company that kept up with industry norms should be, in terms of performance and size. The team went on into a limited, multiple-factor matrix analysis of the business using the operating divisions as the planning units. The team then made its recommendations which included divesting the oldest part of the business on one hand and moving into fast food retailing on the other. While the consultants had carefully pre-sold their ideas to most of the key people on an individual basis, when the senior management met together for the final report, they rejected eighty percent of the recommendations out of hand as unrealistic and not in keeping with the traditions of the company.

As in the case of a planning staff, an outside and/or inside consulting team can serve as a major and cost-effective supporting mechanism to the operating management. But there is a delicate question of who sees him- or herself as the prime architect of the blueprint of the future.

Board of Directors

There is a lot of publicity today suggesting that corporations ought to both expand their boards to include more outsiders and expand the roles played by the board in the affairs of the company. Much of the interest in expanding board membership beyond the old-boy network comes from the emergence of the five Es—environment, energy, equality, ethics, and employment—as areas of corporate responsibility. Wisdom about these matters, however, does not necessarily qualify board members to contribute usefully to strategic planning any more than do having been on the board for years and having great skill in reading financial reports. When the seriousness and depth of thinking required to define planning units and to develop a believable multiple-factor matrix snapshot of a fast-moving emerging company is considered, it seems unlikely that board members who will spend perhaps ten days a year devoted to the enterprise can usefully participate in a process other than reviewing proposed and alternative decisions.

There is a model that is an exception to this, however. Texas Instruments, one of the world's leading new companies, heavily involves its outside board members in various aspects of the company at a rate exceeding thirty days a year. The quality of the people and the familiarity that comes from this extended participation enhances their ability to contribute to the strategic issues confronting this high-growth company.

To conclude this first point about the strategic planning process: The ease of plan implementation is greatly enhanced when the senior line managers of the company are at the center of the entire process.

THE RIGHT PEOPLE, AGENDA, AND INFORMATION

The word *process* suggests a particular method of doing something that generally involved a number of steps or operations done on a continuing basis. The history of strategic planning to date suggests that it becomes more and more valuable as it becomes integrated into the normal flow of events in the company. Here are some of the pitfalls of the past.

Task Forces and Committees

Typically set up on *ad hoc* basis, members of such groups as task forces and committees often have difficulty giving enough time and energy to their project to generate much more than a report. Committee members might be chosen to make up a calendar, but if they are the right people (key line managers) to do the job, they will be stretched to their limits doing both their "regular jobs" and the special assignment.

Management Retreats

It is very tempting to send the hard-driving management of a fast-growing company into the woods or onto a beach for a few days where lofty thoughts and dreams for the future can soar without the pressure of now. There are several drawbacks, however, in addition to the one-time nature of the retreat. Most likely the right people will not be present. The right people for an effective strategic planning process vary over time as different planning units and different issues—competitive position, market attractiveness, for instance, are aired. If the right people are not present, neither will be the right information. The process has broken down before it has started.

Another drawback is the nature of the agenda in a retreat setting. By design, key people are removed from the day-to-day realities, but this placement of strategic planning outside the mainstream of the business gives it an unreal or academic aura.

The management team of a very dynamic San Francisco company removed itself to Pebble Beach for a five-day planning session focused on a three-year plan. The team was accompanied by several consultants and staff people who assisted the CEO and others throughout the week. There was a great deal of discussion in and out of the meeting rooms, and some tentative conclusions were reached regarding future directions. But the spirit of the meeting was best expressed by a senior vice-president who, at the finish of the last scheduled meeting, rose from his place at the green, felt-covered table, rubbed his hands together, and exclaimed with a big smile, "Great! Now let's get back to work!"

The right people, agenda, and information exist physically and psychologically only near the mainstream of the enterprise.

A TIMELY SCHEDULE

There are three major mistakes to avoid concerning timing. The first has already been discussed—namely, that a once-a-year strategic planning effort is unlikely to produce the behaviorial changes needed to execute significant strategic assignments. Strategic change has to be cultivated and grown over time, like asparagus. The second mistake is to couple a new strategic planning effort to an existing planning effort for the next fiscal year. This is done often, but there are at least four major drawbacks to doing so.

- The coupling will encourage extrapolation of current trends and thinking.
- Inadequate time will be given to the type of issues suggested in the previous chapter because the crowded schedule for next year's plan is always a pressing matter.
- Planning units and existing units, if they are not equivalent, will become confused.
- Trade-off decisions about strategic assignments for various planning units will be prematurely caught in the budget battles of the coming year.

In time, an emerging company can have an annual calendar that smoothly sequences both a review of strategic matters and the plans for the coming year. Arriving at that point, however, may take three or four years and a like number of passes at strategic planning, with visible improvement and growth in confidence after each pass.

The third common mistake concerning timing is to entangle strategic planning with budgeting. Budgeting should be one of the last steps in an effective longer-range planning sequence. Here is how such a sequence might go, assuming that there is at least general agreement on a tentative set of objectives for the enterprise:

1. Define the planning units.
2. Prepare a business position "size-up" or audit of each planning unit that includes the following: its historic sales, earnings, growth

rate, and technology trends; its current status in terms of market share and other factors deemed important by the senior management; the outlook to the unit's planning horizon—expected competitive moves, government actions, and so forth; and, finally, what appear to be viable, longer-range alternatives for the unit (what could be done with it) and the projected costs and returns for each alternative.

3. Review the audit of each planning unit. In a series of semiformal meetings, the senior management team should review the audits. As a result of the discussions, a consensus should be reached about where the unit stands competitively now and what the realistic alternatives for the future are. (What *is* the unit? What will or could the unit become if . . . ?)

   At this point it is important to note that the audit will not be repeated in its entirety every planning cycle. But it is necessary to develop an in-depth *point of view* about a unit that is based on sound data collection, analysis, and thinking. Given a point of view, the auditing of future planning cycles will be a matter of updating, confirming, and highlighting changes affecting the unit.

4. Relate the planning units to one another to form a composite view of the enterprise. The planning techniques in the high end of the planning hierarchy can be useful at this point. For example, the multiple-factor matrix shown below can provide the framework for looking at the whole enterprise.

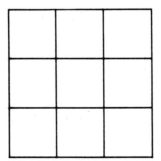

5. Analyze the portfolio of units and possibilities, and decide on the strategic assignments for the various units.

6. Prepare a comprehensive plan for each unit for the chosen planning period. Such a plan would be, essentially, a longer-term blue-

print for achieving specified objectives. Such a plan would cover markets, facilities, people, cash projections, etc., and reflect the unit's strategic assignment.

7. Review and adopt a strategic plan for each unit. In another series of semiformal meetings, the senior management team should review the detailed plans submitted by the people responsible for the units. Revisions based on resource availability and other factors are then made as necessary. The compilation of the unit's strategic plans now becomes the strategic plan for the entire enterprise unless there are new areas of activity to be pursued outside the existing planning-unit structure. This comprehensive plan, based on the audits, now becomes the "living" document, a baseline against which subsequent annual operating plans can be formulated and measured. The sum of the unit plans is top management's road map to the future. Its contents, furthermore, may suggest, at certain junctures, alternative routes—changes to the corporate structure, job assignments, and compensation systems, for example.

8. Prepare, review, and adopt annual operating plans. This step has now most likely become an up-graded or broadened version of the usual budget approval process. The added ingredient is the presence of a strategic plan that serves as the guideline to operating and functional managers.

9. Conduct regular reviews that compare performance to the adopted operating plans.

10. Repeat steps 1–9 in subsequent time periods (redefining the planning units in step 1 and the auditing of step 2 only as judgment dictates).

These ten steps are listed to serve as a general guideline. A balanced, informed point of view has to be formed by the management about each of the vital parts of the company. The parts have to be sorted through systematically and compared. They represent the cards currently in management's hand. Decisions have to be reached about longer-term directions. Assuming that the enterprise has finite resources (not every part of an emerging company can be built successfully, indefinitely), a portfolio of strategies most likely will be required. The process of analysis and reaching decisions is not as rational and not as lockstep as it appears here in print. There is a significant portion of "muddling through." But the fact that muddling occurs does not negate the usefulness of a structured process to a complex, fast-moving company.

DECISIONS THAT COMMIT CASH AND PEOPLE TO MARKETPLACE POSITIONING ASSIGNMENTS EXTENDING BEYOND THE CURRENT OPERATING CYCLE

One excellent test question that helps evaluate the realness of the strategic planning of an emerging company is, Did the management decide it was going to stop doing anything? If the answer is no, chances are the planning process or effort put into it was ineffectual. Particularly in the first few cycles of planning, emerging companies need to discard some of their baggage to release resources for better uses. The "no" test is a handy one.

Another test is whether available money and talent is actually being channeled into the chosen opportunity areas uncovered or confirmed by the strategic effort, or whether the money and talent are still going where it has historically gone—to the squeakiest wheel, or to the particular personal interest of the president, regardless of the realities of the environment in which the company wishes to excel. Intuition is not obsolete, but neither is it immune from examination. Strategic planning, in many respects, is a narrow label for what is really a new process of managing an enterprise in increasingly complex times.

Summary on Planning

8

"In all labor there is profit. But more talk leads
only to poverty."

Proverbs 14:23

The planning part of what the top managers of emerging companies
do grows in importance as the enterprise gathers momentum. Size and
success reduce flexibility; the price of trial-and-error decisions goes up;
and the psychological cost of failure escalates. There is a lot to be said
for aligning the gathering momentum with one or more selected opportunity streams that appear to flow where the stakeholders, in one
way or another, have consciously chosen to go.

Strategic planning, a process of determining in advance the course
of action to which resources will be committed to generate more momentum, has become shrouded in mistique like other management
practices that have come into vogue over the years by the forces of necessity and invention. Mistique is unnecessary. Most any management team that has brought its enterprise through the initial survival
stage, can—given timely, right information—make optimal decisions
for the enterprise. But to get the right information, the right questions
have to be asked.

The kinds of "right questions and issues" have been suggested
here in Section Two. In an enterprise of any complexity, first the natural parts must be identified. What are the important, discrete units of
our business? Top management needs to decide these in the same way
that an artist must decide on the colors to place on his or her pallet.

After the planning units are identified, a point of view about each
one needs to be formulated. Where does this unit stand in relation to
its competition and the projected realities of the market(s) it serves?

Finally, all the units must be compared one to another in the search for a combination of activities that balance risks, potential rewards, and the values of the senior people involved. Discrete planning units are the ingredients of alternative strategic scenarios.

There are a variety of techniques that can be used to reach trade-off decisions. But the real heart of the matter is a process of getting the right people, agenda, and information together on a continuing basis, so they can share and hone their collective wisdom. What other fuel can feed a dynamic business?

The result of an effective strategic-planning *process* is a set of assignments to which the people of the enterprise can respond. If the shop foreman or salesperson or operations supervisor can't understand the assignment, chances are it won't be carried out—for sure, it won't be executed with the desired *élan*.

There is a certain attraction to a completed plan, regardless of its title: corporate, strategic, or whatever. The black-and-white sureness of printed pages, the visual harmony of the charts, matrixes, circles, and pies, and the inherent symmetry of projections all speak to our need for rationality and order; they are perfect products of the professional manager, But "professional" managers in the lawyer/doctor sense don't exist. Managing is a lot more than planning anyhow, and the experienced hand at it knows from the start that the three-ring binder full of rationality and order is an illusion—a necessary illusion, perhaps—but an illusion nonetheless. The results of greatest value derived from an effective strategic-planning process are not those on the printed page, but rather those in the minds of the participants in the process. If the process produces a relatively high degree of enlightened consistency in the attitudes, outlooks, intentions, and ultimately, behavior of the pacesetters of the enterprise, competition watch out! Some ideas that can contribute to this desired consistency are covered in the last section of this book: Beyond Planning.

SECTION THREE
BEYOND PLANNING

The Search for Competitive Advantage

9

"Hit 'em where they ain't."

Dizzy Dean

Building a better mousetrap so the world will beat a path to your door is an integral part of management folklore. "Better" is the key word, for it conveys at once several important points. First, it says that business executives are, of necessity, engaged in a competitive vocation. If a given product or service or enterprise is "better," then another product or service or enterprise is "worse." It is the unit's relative position *vis-a-vis* competition that counts. Recognition of this fact is one reason why the systematic development of information about competitors is on the rise as a corporate activity. It is also responsible for the trend of setting corporate performance objectives (ROI, earnings per share, sales growth, etc.) that are gauged against other companies playing in the same league instead of against absolutes—for example, "Fifteen percent ROI or bust!"

Second, "better" implies that there is incremental value for the ultimate user, not for the R/D department, sales force, or middlemen at intermediate distribution points. It is the world—not your employees or business associates—that is supposed to come down the path to your door. When an enterprise has products or services with better values than its competitors have, and the desired customers give preference to them, the enterprise has developed a competitive advantage. Such advantage typically takes one of four forms.

TECHNICAL SUPERIORITY

The mousetrap that consistently catches more mice with minimal noise, or snap, due to an improved spring design, or one that has more deceptive visual characteristics has a strong chance of doing well in the marketplace if its virtues are adequately communicated. Such technical superiority via engineering and design has been and is the primary method of competing for many product companies in the emerging class. In fact, it was just such technical innovations that fueled much of the boom of the 1960s in the U.S., and the decline in exactly such innovation is identified as one of the major contributors in recent years to the decline in the competitive strength of the U.S. *vis-a-vis* Japan and Germany.

R/D activities normally spawn a large proportion of new commercial products and processes. But as *Business Week* reports in its special issue of June 30, 1980, "The Reindustrialization of America," R/D spending in constant dollars reached a peak in 1968 and has hovered near that level ever since. Another indicator of the declining rate of technical innovation is patent activity. In 1970, more than 76,000 patents were filed. In 1975, the number dropped to 64,000, but the share of U.S. patents granted to foreign nationals in 1975 was 28%—up from 13% in 1966.

The message is clear. At both country and company levels, technical superiority provides a competitive advantage. But, like other directional issues faced by the senior people of fast-growing enterprises, the search for innovative ideas is likely to be futile if it is done faint-heartedly, or on a stop/start basis. The basic kinds of activities needed to produce meaningful innovation require a continuing commitment and a critical mass of appropriately managed talent. Lacking such a commitment, the management of an enterprise had perhaps best look to the other ways to develop a competitive advantage.

QUALITY

The mousetrap that lasts longer and seldom malfunctions will often be worth a premium price to people with mice problems. Many might even "walk a mile" out of the way for the brand of trap with a reputation for being the most reliable. Where does such quality come from? Production expertise is often the key, although design—of either product or manufacturing process—can play a big part. The important point is that quality, like technical superiority, doesn't just happen. If a competitive advantage based on product or service quality is to be developed, it has to be cultivated over time from top to bottom in the organization. For an emerging company, it is often difficult to muster enough resources to, say, vigorously pursue simultaneously both technical superiority and a premium-price niche based on production-related quality. A trade-off has to be made. Is the company's competitive advantage to be built on being first into the marketplace with what is new, or on being second in with less innovation but a more reliable product and shipments that meet delivery promises? Which business value of the product is to be the crucial one? Do plans, strategic and annual, reflect support for whatever decision is made?

SUPPORTING SERVICES

The mousetrap that comes complete with a special cheese, precut in trap-size pieces, a disposal bag for the deceased rodent, and a cassette tape on the art of mice entrapment by Dr. Felix Katt, a famous catcher, may well be a winner in the marketplace—especially if no competitor is providing such help or if the geographic market served has only recently been invaded by mice and there is a felt need for mouse-combat training. Such supporting mechanisms can distinguish a "me-too" product or service from its competitors in ways that produce superior business results.

IBM, almost since its inception, has stressed customer service as *the* guiding star of the company—at the expense of technical superiority if necessary. Such single-mindedness on the part of the management, starting with the founder, has produced a company with a distinct, ingrained, formidable competitive advantage.

Sunset Designs, an emerging company that makes and markets home sewing kits across the U.S., is well known for its originality and freshness of design. In fact, the company employs on either a direct or free-lance basis some of the most outstanding hand-work designers in the country. Yet the top management has consciously decided to build its *primary* competitive advantage on the basis of a broad inventory and quick delivery service to retailers. This choice was made after a lot of head scratching and deliberation about the actual reasons both consumers and retailers buy, and what was required to gain a lasting competitive advantage in an industry characterized by many small, cottage-type competitors. The capital required to build a sophisticated inventory and order-processing system capable of shipping out the incoming orders within twenty-four hours was large enough to be beyond the reach of most of the competitors. And the resulting system does, in fact, move the high-demand items onto retailers' shelves in a fraction of the time it has historically taken. Everyone comes out ahead—except for Sunset Design's competitors.

PRICE

The mousetrap that is least expensive may well sell best in established, mature markets. Low price may or may not be tied to low quality. Texas Instruments has built a number of successful businesses with excellent products mass-produced with the objective of achieving the lowest cost per unit. At Dana Corporation, a mammoth manufacturer of medium-technology mechanical products, the theme for years has been productivity improvement. The company has doubled its productivity in the last seven years—a period during which the output per hour worked for all companies in the U.S. increased only an average of 0.7% per year. Increased productivity yielding a competitive advantage based on price is a viable objective for a management to espouse if the enterprise has enough value-added to work with, and if the desired buyers are particularly price conscious.

Which of the four avenues are likely to be most productive in the search for competitive advantage? For an emerging company, the most attractive avenue is often the one least traveled. It is clear from studies of companies with long-term success patterns that few of them can excel *vis-a-vis* competition in more than one way. The company with technical superiority will seldom have the lowest priced products; the company with a reputation for service and support ("We service what we sell.") will often not be the premium-priced, quality giant in the industry. It's very difficult to be all things to all people; and its even more difficult to get the hard-driving officers of growth companies to give more than lip service to this fact and its corollary that, therefore, the enterprise has to pick and choose what it will be, to whom. A July 21, 1980 article in *Business Week* entitled "Putting Excellence Into Management" (see Reading IV) put the matter well in that it described eight attributes that characterize the managements of thirty-seven companies considered "well managed" by observers of U.S. business. One of those attributes was deep management concentration on one key business value. To stress one value above others requires discipline and conviction. The conviction can often flow from the strategic planning process.

In essence, the search for competitive advantage is the search for the one thing the company will do better than anyone else. Finding a niche and filling it is a variation on building a better mousetrap that also ranks high in the folklore popularity polls. Identification of better-mousetrap opportunities and niches comes from a thorough knowledge and understanding of the field in which an enterprise competes. The multiple-factor matrix approach described in Chapter 6 included such competitive considerations as ease of market entry and the number and size of major competitors. But the important issue of a discrete competitive advantage can be lost or buried in the mass of more statistical data if management is not alert.

It's hard to quantify the value of an existing or potential competitive edge in selected products or markets. What's the dollar value of, say, 3,000 employees who, throughout each working day, all think about productivity or customer service or quality? Hard to say. What's the value of a competitive advantage? What does it take to get one? It seems clear that to "get one" takes a concerned effort focused on a single business value–not to the exclusion of other values—but as the capstone to a solid strategic plan.

Cultivating a Corporate Culture

10

"Culture is not in the job; it is in the attitude to the job."

C. Alphonso Smith

In the 1950s and early 1960s, managing by objectives, MBO, was "the thing." Then strategic planning moved to center stage and commanded the spotlight, a position it still holds. Waiting in the wings today is the next star, corporate culture. The term culture conveys an array of meanings: closeness, shared values, common language, individual identification with a larger body and, usually, a degree of mutual respect among its membership. There is a tribe-like character about the term. And the characteristics of a tribe are, in fact, what the occupants of an increasing number of executive suites see as a desirable goal for their organizations. The *inability to implement* strategic plans is one of the driving forces behind the growing interest in cultivating a corporate culture. Reading V, a cover article from *Business Week*, attests to arrival of the next star in the executive suite for the 1980s.

Consider the typical sequence in a strategic-planning effort. Ideally, there is a planning process built around the firm's line management. This process at some point produces a plan that usually involves moving away from some old products or, perhaps, markets and into some new ones. Such moves require changes in behavior. Now the question arises as to how best to spread the word about the plan and the determination to carry it out so that the enterprise does, in fact, change direction *X* degrees and take a new course into the future. In short, how is the plan to be implemented?

Budget decisions—allocating and withholding money—and top job assignments are, of course, the first line of implementation. Money and manpower are given to those parts of the business to be "built." And top management can pretty well call the shots on these matters of cash and bosses. The next level of implementation is more difficult, however, as the challenge is now how to reach more deeply into the organization and effectively influence behavior there. The traditional method is to communicate with the broader corporate population through some assortment of meetings, manuals, and memos, and then to follow up over time with reports and reviews that result in rewards and admonitions as appropriate. This sequence is a model of a fairly standard approach used by modern managers in the Western industrialized countries. It is an approach that has its limitations; and it is not the only approach available. Consider the limitations first.

The traditional system of encouraging desired behavior in organizations of any size and complexity requires a web of supporting information systems and control/performance review procedures that attempt to inform, monitor, and influence the day-to-day actions of individuals. In effect, regardless of the size of the human relations component included, such systems attempt to direct what people do from the outside. And no matter how good the system is, chances are it will reach its capacity for influencing behavior beyond the perfunctory level once there are more than 200 or 300 *key* individuals (managers and supervisors) involved. Beyond that point, at least for companies still in the early stages of construction, alternatives to elaborate systems of external control to influence behavior should probably be considered. One such alternative is a style of managing aimed at internalizing in its population the enterprise's values. Instead of using speeches, the company newsletter, and bulletin boards to force-feed information on company objectives, strategies, competitive theme, and so forth, an attempt is made to give each individual his or her own internal guidance system. Such an attempt is a process usefully called the cultivation of a corporate culture.

The leading research on this subject started with an analysis of the similarities of and differences between American and Japanese managing styles. Japan has an industrial history in its larger enterprises that emphasizes long-term employment and company loyalty. A few years ago an academic question arose as to whether the rapid industrialization of Japan and its increased contact with the West would force significant alterations in the traditional Japanese management style. For example, would Japanese executives gravitate toward Western practices? A companion question was whether traditional U.S. practices, based on high growth and mobility and low levels of company loyalty or identification, might have to change with the slowdown in economic expansion and the gradual closing of the domestic frontiers that began in the 1960s.

Some of the original research undertaken on the question uncovered evidence that, rather than changing, the Japanese were successfully exporting a number of their management practices to their manufacturing and distribution companies in the U.S. The opposite was not true, however. U.S. managers did not successfully export their practices to their operations in Japan. More important, other related research on the broader aspects of modern managing styles uncovered evidence that at least in the faster growing, higher technology U.S. companies examined, the more successful ones were those whose management practices or "climates" had a lot of Japanese flavor. And it was the Japanese flavor that seemed to cause such work-force attributes as shared values, company loyalty, identification with the success of the company, and so forth. The research also found that these attributes tended to be internalized in the employees of a given company, as in a culture.

The researchers, Bill Ouchi in particular, crystallized seven distinct elements of what was labeled a mixed or "Modified American" management style that seemed to utilize the best from both the East and the West, and which had, in fact, been developed in some leading American companies over a number of years. To quote from one of Ouchi's articles:*

> Some American companies, by reputation, have many of the characteristics of this mixed model. Best known are Kodak, Cummins Engine, IBM, Levi Strauss, National Cash Register, Procter and Gamble, Utah International, and Minnesota Mining and Manufacturing (3M). In each case, the historic rates of turnover are low, loyalty and morale are reputed to be very high, and identification with the company is reputed to be strong. In addition, each company has been among the most successful of American companies for many decades, a record that strongly suggests that something about the form of organization, rather than solely a particular product or market position, has kept the organization vital and strong.

To paraphrase Ouchi's comments elsewhere in the same article, which is included as Reading VI in this book, the research gives evidence that although present-day Americans probably do not want to return to old-style paternalism, they favor a work organization that provides associational ties, stability, and job security. The Japanese-American mixed form may simultaneously permit individual freedom and group cohesion in work organizations that are managed in such a way as to put back together a social fabric that used to be made up of

---

*William G. Ouchi and Alfred M. Jaeger, "Type Z Organization: A Corporate Alternative to Village Life," *Stanford Business School Alumni Bulletin*, Fall 1977–78, p. 15.

neighbors, family, church, and school chums, but that has been torn apart over time by industrialization, urbanization, mobility, and the division of labor into smaller and smaller pieces.

To weave such a fabric requires a basic commitment on senior management's part to make the enterprise more than just a place to work. A culture takes time and energy to create—*and* declared values to share. Survival, as a business, is often a useful common value and cohesive element during the early years of an emerging company. But success tends to wear these away, too frequently leaving a vacuum. What were exciting, fulfilling crusades become just jobs. And real pluses like low turnover rate, high productivity gains, and stimulating *espirit de corps* settle down to the norms for the area or industry. This sequence *is* avoidable, but it takes an investment.

From the work of Ouchi and his colleagues on the Modified American style, there appear to be four characteristics that have particular relevance to emerging companies. These characteristics identify the pots into which the required investment of money and management energy must be poured.

CONSENSUAL DECISION-MAKING

Used here, this term is not just a variation on participatory management in which everyone involved gets to say something before the most senior person announces his or her decision. In consensual decision-making the manager will not decide nonroutine matters until he or she has fully heard the ideas and opinions of those affected. Often, in this approach, the "best" solution seems to float gradually to the surface, a joint product of those involved. And even if it doesn't, and the senior person finally does call the play, so to speak, support for that decision is likely to be broader than if it were made unilaterally. This characteristic, in many respects, is an extension of the managing-versus-doing perspective to be discussed in Chapter 11. A manager can afford the psychological cost of giving up some of his or her perceived power to make decisions only if he or she sees the job of managing as one of achieving results through others.

IMPLICIT, INFORMAL CONTROLS WITH EXPLICIT, FORMALIZED MEASURES RESULTING IN SLOW EVALUATION AND PROMOTION

Nowhere is the line of demarcation between Western and Eastern styles so clear as in the area of controls. The typical Western style features hard, measurable, dated objectives against which individuals are measured and rewarded or punished. The typical Eastern style is often portrayed as an invisible, apparently semisocial process of evaluating individual contributions over what seems like an eternity. It is a worthy challenge to develop a hybrid style, and just such a hybrid is found in the successful companies considered by the researchers to have distinct, positive, corporate cultures. To quote Drs. Ouchi and Jaeger:

> The speed with which evaluation and promotion of individuals take place is self-explanatory, but its effects are subtle. If promotion is rapid, managers at any given level of the organization will be less completely socialized into the organizational culture than if promotion is slow. It follows that if the organization has had a history of rapid promotion for many years, it will not have as unified an atmosphere as will an organization with slower rates of upward mobility.
>
> In addition to the effects on the atmosphere of an organization, the speed of evaluation has significant effects upon the character of interpersonal relationships. In an achievement-oriented organization, evaluations of performance must be free of dimensions which are not related to achievement. Specifically, friendship and kinship must be explicitly prohibited as criteria of evaluation. The supervisor can never know whether his or her evaluation of a subordinate is tinged with personal likes or dislikes if there is any personal attachment. The only solution open to this evaluator is an impersonal relationship. If evaluations occur rapidly, for example once each six months, only the direct supervisor will be charged with the responsibility of rendering the evaluation, and he or she is thus blocked from forming personal, friendship ties with the subordinate.
>
> If major evaluations occur only once every five or ten years, however (as is common in Japanese firms), then the evaluation is no longer explicitly rendered by one superior but rather emerges through a non-explicit process of agreement between the many superiors who know the subordinate. Under this condition, the direct superior is freed from the need to preserve an "objective" attitude toward the subordinate and thus can take a personal interest in him or her. Under rapid evaluation, therefore, the formation of personal ties is much less likely to occur than under slow evaluation.*

It is easy to visualize how, through practices such as these, a culture is gradually developed. Some readers may react that the end product of the process might be more than a little dull! But the evidence is that if all the ingredients suggested here are present, along with the kind of systematic planning process outlined in earlier chapters, the result is a collection of qualified, dedicated people consciously going somewhere together.

---

*Op. Cit., p. 16.

MODERATELY SPECIALIZED CAREER PATH

In the typical Western company, the ambitious upcomer will normally remain in a functional specialty—marketing, production, or finance, for instance—for a large portion of his or her career. There is evidence that although such specialization may produce a high level of professionalism, it also results in a low level of loyalty to the enterprise; it is primarily the professionals that skip regularly from company to company.

At the other extreme is the typical Eastern company in which the upcomer is moved over time through various parts or departments of the company, and thereby develops a specialized knowledge of the company itself, as well as a web of personal relationships throughout the organization. Specialization on the company, of course, reduces the likelihood of job-hopping and may result in a certain inbred quality that, at the extreme, is stifling. Hence the phrase, *moderately* specialized career path, which suggests that a mixture of functional, as well as company specialization, may be the proper blend for the upcomers in an expanding company.

LONG-TERM EMPLOYMENT

Long-term employment would appear to be self-explanatory, but the implications run deep. Responsible employees who have been in a company for an extended period know how to get things done. This is especially true for those who have worked in a variety of assignments. An organization of people who know how to get the right things done by working together is more than likely going to have an efficiency advantage over its less cohesive competitors.

It is standard practice for corporate officials to espouse employment stability, yet it is quite something else to espouse long-term employment as an explicit objective, if not a responsibility, of the enterprise. And such acceptance has a number of strings attached, a major one being a concern for each employee's total well-being—work, family, health, and development. A number of the younger electronics companies in California's silicon valley are experimenting with ways to broaden the umbrella over their employees—from providing the simple physical amenities like jogging tracks and exercise rooms to encouraging senior people to develop a continuing and widening familiarity with the broader aspects of their subordinates' lives. Such social initiatives may sound unduly foreign, but the reader must consider whether the pace and mobility of the times don't require some fresh approaches to making organizations work—especially organizations that are still in formative stages today.

To conclude this brief sojourn into the realm of cultivating a corporate culture: The ultimate target is an enlightened one, namely longer-range, product/market positioning plans for the enterprise *that get implemented.* Implementation grows tougher with the increases in a company's size and complexity that usually accompany its success. At some point, formal information and control systems reach their practical limits in spurring people on to above-average output and achievement. External guidance systems need to be supplemented—or perhaps replaced—by internal guidance systems. No emerging company grows up without generating a culture. The issue is whether the cultural norms are arrived at by conscious cultivation or by default.

Managing   11
Versus
Doing

"Behind an able man there are always other able men."

Chinese Proverb

The preceding chapters of this book suggest a heavy menu of activities for senior managers. Most of the activities do not pay off immediately. Time spent on such activities—at the expense of those that have an immediate payoff or impact—is often hard to justify. The executive in an emerging company needs a point of view about these new activities required of him or her, and a way of differentiating them from the less abstract ones that probably led to accolades in the past. That point of view can usefully be developed by acquiring a handy way to distinguish between managing and other kinds of work.

Managing is a distinct *kind* of work. It is different from nonmanaging work—not better, not superior, but different. Without a practical point of view about how managing differs from other work, it is unlikely that the ideas about strategic planning presented in this book— or ideas about any serious material on other managing subjects—will be applied. After finishing a book such as this, or a seminar, or a film, busy executives will rub their hands together, nod their heads affirmatively, and then "get back to work" doing precisely what they were doing before the enriching educational experience. The fault does not lie entirely with the book's author, the teacher, or the executive; the fault is evenly divided and reflects both a semantic problem and a lack of perspective on everyone's part.

Here is a very short story followed by an equally short exercise to

illustrate the point. The Head Ski Company* is one of the all-time fa-
vorite business policy cases used in graduate classrooms across the
country. Howard Head was an engineer/inventor when in 1950 he
founded his company to introduce metal skis to the world. By 1965,
Head Ski was the U.S. market leader in the sale of high-priced metal
skis. As President, Howard Head had led his company through a number of ups and downs over its fifteen-year history, but in 1965 the company was well-positioned in a solid market and had plenty of cash and
a high price/earnings (P/E) ratio on its publicly traded stock. At that
time, various expansion moves were being considered by the senior
management team of the Head Ski Company. The President's day was
filled with a variety of activities. Which of them were managing activities, and which were actually non-managing activities? You decide.
Check your answer.

EXERCISE

Was Howard Head managing when he . . .

	Yes	No
1. Spent an afternoon with the President of a retail chain of stores, Head Ski's largest customer?	___	___
2. Solved a knotty design problem that had been perplexing his chief engineer for several weeks?	___	___
3. Visited the senior loan officer of the bank where the company did business to negotiate a loan?	___	___
4. Discussed with a European consultant a range of fabrics and colors for a new product line of Head Ski clothing that was under consideration?	___	___
5. Gave a speech to a noon gathering of stock analysts in New York City?	___	___
6. Took his regular walking tour through the plant in order to keep in touch with the people and processes?	___	___
7. Held a staff meeting with the officers of the Company to review cash-flow projections?	___	___
8. Interviewed several final job candidates for the position of controller, and made an offer to one of them?	___	___
9. Accompanied a recently promoted Vice-President of Sales to a national sporting goods convention in order		

*"Head Ski Company, Inc.," a Harvard Business School case distributed by the Intercol-
legiate Case Clearing House, Boston.

to get the VP off to a good start with some of the industry's old timers?   ___   ___

10. Initiated an open discussion of corporate objectives at the regular Board of Directors meeting?   ___   ___

Before reviewing the ten activities one by one, think about these issues that can usefully flow from the exercise.

I.   What are the implications to the Head Ski Company if Howard Head, on taking the same exercise, were to answer yes to all ten?

II. If Howard Head were to answer yes to all ten, how would most of the other officers of his company probably answer to similar lists of their activities?

III. With all the senior people at Head Ski so busy with the kinds of activities listed, what kinds of things are most likely *not* getting done?

IV. What must happen at Head Ski Company if the enterprise is to keep on succeeding?

Starting from the bottom with issue IV, it will be clear to most experienced hands that what the company needs if it is to continue to lead the parade in its industry is a well thought-out plan that provides for a continuing flow of new products and talent, a control/reporting system to keep track of the expanding empire, and so forth. *Rationally*, those needs are obvious to any practiced business executive. *Rationally*, they are also obvious to Howard Head and his team members. But in practice, according to the case, how does President Head, at least, spend most of his time? Look back at the Exercise.

1. Was the President "managing" during that afternoon with the company's largest customer? No, he was selling. Selling isn't managing.

2. Was the President managing as he worked out the solution to the engineering problem? No, he was doing engineering work. Engineering isn't managing.

3. Was Howard Head managing when he visited the bank to negotiate loan arrangements? No, he was doing the technical work of an individual executive. Financing isn't managing.

"Now wait a minute," you say, "all of those activities are part of Mr. Head's job. They have to be done. He *has* to do them! Who's kidding whom, here?" And you are partially right—the jobs do have to be done. Whether Mr. Head's time is best spent on them is a separate question. Here's where point of view or perspective enters the picture.

Every senior manager is faced with a variety of tasks that, typically, consume all of his or her available time.

100% OF AVAILABLE TIME

In the absence of an easy way to differentiate managing work from nonmanaging work, the nonmanaging activities (selling, engineering, negotiating, etc.) will almost always usurp the managing work for the following reasons:

- The manager has historically excelled in the specific nonmanagement activities. His or her success at performing as an individual probably led to a promotion with managing-level responsibility.
- A nonmanagement activity is often spontaneous. It arises naturally, without being initiated or cultivated. The phone rings, the mail arrives, or a subordinate asks for help: And PRESTO, there's a chance to make an individual contribution.
- A nonmanagement activity usually leads to a clean result. An order is won or lost. A problem is solved. A loan is signed. The audience applauds.

As a practical matter, *nonmanaging work is the work of an individual.* When Mr. Head is selling, or engineering, or negotiating, he is "doing," that is, working to achieve a result by himself. And "doing" work with the momentum of personal history behind it and the high potential for immediate feedback and results has a proven capability to overshadow—push aside—managing work.

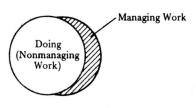

100% OF AVAILABLE TIME

In the words of Louis A. Allen,

When called upon to perform management work and technical work during the same time period, a manager will tend to give first priority to technical work.*

What is this managing work that so easily gets pushed aside or, at least, ends up being crammed into the time left over at the end of a week, month, or budget cycle? A number of authors have crystalized definitions over the years, but Ray Loen perhaps captures it best:

*It may be helpful for you to think of planning as **developing your plan**, directing as **implementing your plan**, and controlling as **seeing your plan was carried out**—in each instance through your people.†*

In short, managing is achieving planned results through others. This doesn't mean *with* others, or *for* others, but *through* others in the same way that a football coach is responsible for touchdowns: When he's coaching, he isn't carrying the ball, blocking, or catching a pass. To get the job done, he is selecting, motivating, evaluating, gathering and processing information, and conferring with his team.

Few executives, if any, can spend full time managing—coaching their teams. Most all are faced with the challenge of being player/ coach. On occasion Howard Head *did* need to visit his company's largest customer and sell. No argument. But he wasn't managing when he did so! Moral: If all of a CEO's time is spent *doing*, the company's chance of continuing to succeed goes way down. What is needed is balance—balance between time spent on managing and time spent doing the work of an individual. Balance is what is needed, but what's the proper mix?

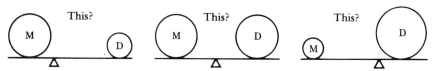

The right mix for any given individual will vary with his or her level of responsibility in the organization, as well as with the size and complexity of the organization. But the tendencies are clear. The

---

*Louis A. Allen. *Professional Management: New Concepts and Proven Practices* (New York: McGraw-Hill, 1973), p. 60.
†Raymond O. Loen. *Manage More by Doing Less* (New York: McGraw-Hill, 1971), p. 8.

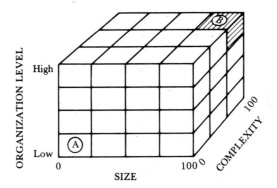

NEED FOR EFFECTIVE MANAGING

larger and more complex the enterprise, the more critical it is for the senior managers to consciously spend increasing amounts of their time managing—achieving planned results through others. The diagram above, Need for Effective Managing, illustrates the idea. The Head Ski Company was somewhere in the center of the cube. Emerging companies tend to gravitate from point A toward point B. Along the way, managing practices must change if the enterprise is to continue succeeding.

Does all this effort to differentiate managing from nonmanaging have any payoff? It is the author's firm opinion that without such differentiation, the chances of the reader actually applying the ideas on strategic planning covered in this book will be slim. And the same goes for ideas on delegating, motivating, organizational structure, performance reviewing, and most of the other "softer" managing subjects that are preached incessantly from seminar pulpits.

Here is another way to visualize the "mix."

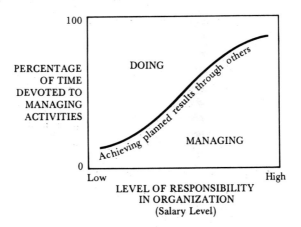

In most organizations, as an individual's salary level increases, the amount of energy allocated to managing activities should probably increase. (The exception to this would be in organizations with dual promotion ladders: a ladder for managers and another for individual contributors such as scientists or salesmen.)

Let's return to the Exercise. Activities 1, 2, and 3 have been discussed. In each instance, Howard Head was doing the work of an individual contributor. He was not achieving results through others. The point is not whether he should or should not be seeing the customer, solving the engineering problem, or negotiating the loan. Perhaps he should. And the same goes for activities 4 and 5—selecting new products and giving speeches. The point is that while Mr. Head may feel compelled to do these things, he's not managing when he is. And if all the officers are following his lead, the emerging Head Ski Company, in the case, is going to stop succeeding and be bypassed by the company's more astute competitors.

Activities 6 and 7 in the Exercise are in a grey zone. Certainly keeping in touch with the organization through tours and meetings may be managing as defined here. It depended on Howard Head's (or any manager's) intentions. Is the activity inspired by a desire to help various subordinates grow, develop, and be bigger people? Or is the manager merely showing the colors and letting the workers know that the ace problem-solver and source of wisdom is still around and working?

Activities 8, 9, and 10 have to do with achieving results through others, and they are representative of the kinds of activities to which the key people in emerging companies must willingly shift a good part of their time and energy. Great companies have been built by single individuals in the past. And there will be others in the 1980s and 1990s. But the percentage is small now and dropping—for reasons outlined in Chapter 3 on how companies grow.

In conclusion, four issues were raised directly following the management-activity exercise. Issues I and II revolved around the implications to the Head Ski Company if its President and other officers all answered yes to all items on the list. The implications pertain to the president and officers of all emerging companies: The job of *managing* a company must get done or a company will peak out at a point equal to the sum of its individuals' efforts. There will be little synergism, and, in an industry with smart competition, Head Ski and companies like it will lose position. The companies will cease to emerge.

Issues III and IV ask, in essence, What is it that will not get done that should be done? The subject of managing is an evolving one, and it can be and has been broken down in numerous ways. Fifty years ago, in the 1930s, you knew about general managing in a progressive company if you understood industrial engineering, accounting, and sales. That was the start of what was then termed scientific management. In the 1940s, some knowledge of human relations came to be required of management as the result of various scientific experiments that unexpectedly uncovered the fact that the output of employees was not merely a physical given. There were psychological aspects to running companies: People could be motivated. Managing became a broader subject.

In the 1950s and 1960s, other functional specialities were added to the list of things the general manager needed to know, or at least to understand. First, marketing came into the limelight as a subject that was more than just a summation of advertising, salesmanship, and pricing. Marketing was followed by breakthroughs in techniques of financial analysis and reporting, and the busy executive had some more functional knowledge to absorb. But something more important happened than these breakthroughs during this period. The idea of managing as a distinct body of knowledge worthy of study (like law or accounting or marketing) gathered momentum. The rapid expansion of the economy in the 1960s, along with the rapid growth in most all domestic institutions such as corporations, universities, and governments, generated a large demand for more managers. Managing by objectives was introduced and commercialized by a number of consultants; it was the first "pure" managing subject to gain a wide exposure and following.

Meanwhile, in the schools of business around the country, certain faculty members were drawing together the threads of thought about managing that ran back in time to earlier thinkers on the subject, from the classical (management process) school associated with Henri Foyol (1841–1925), through the behavioral or human-relations school given visibility by Elton Mayo (1880–1949), to the quantitative school of more recent vintage. Managing was, indeed, a distinct and expanding kind of work.

The result? Today, the idea of managing as a separate discipline worthy of study is well established. There seems to be growing agreement that the subject can be usefully broken down into such major subjects as

Planning   Organizing   Directing   Controlling   Leading

This author prefers the following organization of the subject, but recognizes that any broad-based agreement on how best to organize the field will have to wait for the emergence of a professional association akin to the legal, medical, and accounting associations that have risen to positions of influence in the last fifty years.

Planning	Supervising	Controlling
Objectives	Organizing	Standards
Strategies	Staffing	Performance measurement
Policies	Developing	Performance evaluation
Structure	Leading	
Programs	Motivating	
Procedures	Communicating	
Budgets		

This breakdown of the discipline of managing is not intended to be exhaustive, but rather reasonably comprehensive. Suffice it to say that a manager effective in the fifteen subject areas in the preceding table will most likely do well in achieving planned results through others. The *Planning, Supervising,* and *Controlling* categories are aimed at providing a useful framework for new knowledge. For example, new interviewing techniques fit handily into the Staffing subject area under *Supervising.* Performance evaluation, a hot subject for the 1980s, falls into both Standards under *Controlling* and Developing under *Supervising.* Most of this book is concerned with just two of the *Planning* subjects: Objectives and Strategies.

A reasonably refined point of view on what is and is not managing is important—perhaps even critical—to the top management of companies on the go in competitive industries. It is quite possible, in fact, to make managing a significant part of a company's competitive edge. For a results-through-others orientation tends to result in dynamic plans that have their implementation built in from the start. And implementation is the target. Blueprints that don't result in a house are of little value to a builder or property owner. More often than not, to continue the metaphor, carpenters who used to build rectangular houses with 90° corners are, in the future, going to have to build houses with 100° corners—or maybe no corners at all! Likewise, what people will be doing in companies successful in adapting to changing times will be different in very important ways from what they have done in the past. The capabilities of an enterprise will have been and must be transformed over time. Such a transformation can come about through a crisis, or through thoughtful pressure by the executive team of an organization. If such concern beyond mere planning exists in the minds of the team, and if it is willing to invest in a continuing capability transformation, that team of executives can be said to be practicing strategic management.

Strategic Management in Emerging Companies   **12**

"Parties who want milk should not seat
themselves on a stool in the middle of a field in
hopes that the cow will back up to them."
Elbert Hubbard

New management buzzwords have, in general, a history something like this. A term is conceived, proclaimed orally and in writing, picked up by consultants, academics, and a few astute managerial teams near in proximity and/or philosophy to its progenitor, generalized beyond its original application, overused, and—finally—just plain misused to the point where it passes, muddled, into the etymological swamp in which most companies fish. The terms *planning, strategic planning, corporate culture,* and in time, *strategic management* will all travel this route. A company successful in emerging in the 1980s against larger, entrenched, multifaceted giants and smaller, more specialized competitors will be an early contributor to the swamp, not a late-arriving fisher.

Strategic management is one of the terms listed above. It is generally credited to H. Igor Ansoff.* It implies, on the surface, a set of managing practices that somehow link the day-to-day operations of an enterprise to the planning and decision making that must accompany longer time horizons. Below the surface, in its fullest meaning, the term *strategic management* suggests a state of affairs in which all the members of a dynamic organization move as one in response to plans made, opportunities, and threats—like a flock of migrating birds winging a

---

*See H. Igor Ansoff, R.P. Declerck and R.L. Hayes, *From Strategic Planning to Strategic Management* (New York: John Wiley & Sons, 1976), p. 4.

twisting course across the sky in what appears to be perfectly synchronous, almost effortless motion.

How does an interested CEO or excutive team get strategic management? What are the steps to achieve a state in a company in which all the parts of the organization move with the matched precision of a flight of migrating birds or the best of the professional basketball teams or the finest *corps de ballet?* Some of the ingredients have been suggested earlier in this book: a common vocabulary, a planning process, conscious consideration of the concept of a culture, and perspective about managing, as opposed to doing, work. These elements don't define strategic management or its apparent benefits; neither do they reveal *in toto* how to get there. Suffice it to say that few companies today can usefully serve as models, but there is a growing recognition in management circles that there is a lot more to continuing to succeed than just planning techniques. The consultants at McKinsey & Company, Inc. have developed one view of the sequence involved in moving from a budgeting orientation towards strategic managing. Their thinking is illustrated in Phases in Evolution of Strategic Decision Making* on the next page.

The value system, shown across the bottom of the illustration (from meeting the budget to collectively creating the future), describes the mind set the leaders must have according to this useful view of how strategic management can evolve in a company.

Now, rather than trying any further to define strategic management in combinations of words or pictures, it is possible to consider how an emerging company might operate if it had—by whatever means—arrived at that state of existence labeled strategic management. Here are six characteristics the careful observer of the strategically managed enterprise of the future might discern:

1. A widespread respect for and sensitivity to the environment—particularly the needs of present and potential customers.
2. A well-understood and accepted calendar of events that guarantees top management a "window" on the key issues and operations of the company.
3. A responsive openness among management and supervisory people that reflects a sense of permanency, identification with the company, and even a sense of shared destiny.
4. A relatively subtle and long-term oriented control, reward, and

---

*Frederick W. Gluck, Stephen P. Kaufman, and A. Steven Walleck, "The Evolution of Strategic Management," *McKinsey Staff Paper,* October 1978, p. 4.

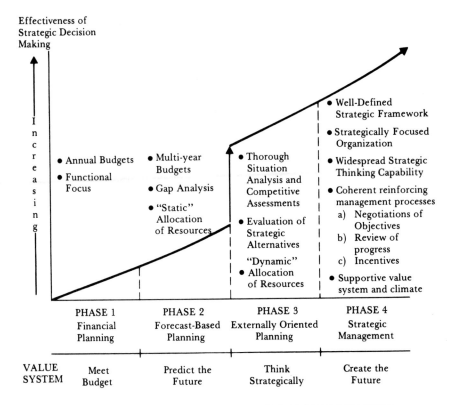

Effectiveness of
Strategic Decision
Making

I
n
c
r
e
a
s
i
n
g

PHASE 1	PHASE 2	PHASE 3	PHASE 4
Financial Planning	Forecast-Based Planning	Externally Oriented Planning	Strategic Management

VALUE SYSTEM	Meet Budget	Predict the Future	Think Strategically	Create the Future

PHASES IN EVOLUTION OF STRATEGIC DECISION MAKING

punishment system that focuses attention on a few major variables and allows wide latitude in day-to-day operations.

5. A well orchestrated, albeit lean, "farm system" for developing both the managing and doing talent vital to the future.

6. An entrepreneurial, "can-do" attitude that seems to acknowledge the temporary nature of today's products or services and market definitions, and to assume with confidence that necessary, informed risks should and can be taken to ensure the continued success of the enterprise.

A detailed consideration of these six characteristics follows.

A widespread respect for and sensitivity to the environment—particularly the needs of present and potential customers. It's not particularly unusual for ninety percent of the non-sales force personnel of an organization to give virtually zero attention or even thought to those who are paying the bills. Even in many service businesses which should presumably know better, customers are typically treated as abstractions rather than people. Yet sensitivity to the needs of the buyers or users, as well as to the other environmental factors that make up the external reality, is the mark of a company that tends to land on its feet regardless of changes in the economy, competitive moves, and social trends in general. Such a consciousness is not bred with a few wall posters exalting the customer. Personal contact is probably the most efficient single method. The controller or line foreman who visits a complaining customer's facility for a first hand exposure to the wrath returns a wiser team member. The company whose officers each spend a minimum of a day a month in the field is going to make more informed decisions today about questions that result in tomorrow.

In a short publication entitled, *The Ten Commandments for Managing a Young Growing Business,** Commandment II is as follows:

Define the business of the enterprise in terms of what is to be bought, precisely by whom, and why.

Businesses are organs of society that perform tasks associated with providing most goods and services the public decides it wishes to own and use. Under this capitalistic system, a business can prosper to the extent it performs its particular tasks effectively and efficiently within the law. The nature of the tasks to be performed usually changes over time as those served change. The successful company predicts and responds to its chosen customers' needs. Customers, therefore, define the business. At all times, some customers are growing in their ability to buy; others are declining. The astute manager ascertains which is which.

How many of your key, nonsalespeople spend a significant percentage of their time in the field?

A well-understood and accepted calendar of events that guarantees top management a "window" on the key issues and operations of the company. As discussed in Chapter 3, one of the prices of success in an emerging company is that the people with the best noses for the action get promoted farther and farther from it as the company prospers. The ace salesperson is elevated to district manager; the sharpest programmer

---

*Steven C. Brandt, "The Ten Commandments for Managing a Young Growing Business," published by the U. S. Management Development Corp., Palo Alto, California.

rises to department head; the strongest person technically becomes president. This is not a formula for the long-term success of the enterprise! It is, in fact poison, with the only proven antidote a process that systematically forces important issues and operations to the surface in manageable pieces. The elements of such processes have been described in this book: planning units, sorting techniques, the primacy of line management, etc. Do the officers of your enterprise have something approaching a finger-tip familiarity with each of the major components of the enterprise?

A responsive openness among management and supervisory people that reflects a sense of permanency, identification with the company, and even a sense of shared destiny. That one should have a sense of destiny with one's company may seem a little idealistic to the casual reader, but companies emerging from an entrepreneurial base have often arrived at that point of success by antics characteristic of "driven" men and women—people with a destiny. Otherwise the long hours, nervous energy, and explosive creativeness just wouldn't have happened. Extending the exciting early-days flavor is one of the great challenges in the category Beyond Planning.

A responsive openness is something that must come from inside people. Psychologists say that it can occur only in an atmosphere from which fear is absent. Fear of what? Fear of mistakes, censure, or even failure in an organizational sense. If an atmosphere exists in which there is a low tolerance for fresh ideas, dissent, or contrary opinions, then the veins of available human resources are going to be mined at the surface only. And the boss—every boss—is the reference point. He or she establishes and reinforces the working atmosphere, for better or worse.

What about identification with the enterprise, a no-no since the nonentity, man-in-the-grey-flannel-suit notoriety of the 1950s? Those who deride the idea of such identification are missing a modern opportunity. Consider this quotation taken from the research on Type Z organizations and corporate culture covered in Chapter 10.

Now all the evidence of psychiatry . . . shows that membership in a group sustains a man, enables him to maintain his equilibrium under the ordinary shocks of life, and helps him to bring up children who will in turn be happy and resilient. If his group is shattered around him, if he leaves a group in which he was a valued member, and if, above all, he finds no new group to which he can relate himself, he will under stress, develop disorders of thought, feeling, and behavior . . . The cycle is vicious; loss of group membership in one generation may make men less capable of group membership in the next. The civilization that, by its very process of growth, shatters small group life will leave men and women lonely and unhappy.

George C. Homans, *The Human Group**

Has your organization progressed beyond bulletin board notices and an annual party or picnic toward establishing a minisociety in which the participants are also contributors?

A relatively subtle and long-term oriented control, reward, and punishment system that focuses attention on a few major variables and allows wide latitude in day-to-day operations. It is common knowledge today that longer range, more strategic plans supported by compensation systems based on this year's ROI, are plans that will probably not be realized. Some authorities even credit the lack of imagination and the high degree of "todayness" in most corporate compensation schemes with the U.S. decline in productivity and innovation. The manager rewarded only for this year's results is going to concentrate on them—at the expense, often, of next year's. This problem can be particularly acute in rapidly growing companies where it is easy to delay investments in information systems, management development, cost controls, and other matters that don't demand immediate attention—where it is easy to delay such investments *until* . . .

There is, and will be a stability in strategically managed companies that breeds the kind of *company* loyalty and dedication most executives deem desirous. It is the kind of loyalty that overrides the trade, professional, or educational parochialism that is sometimes found, for example, in computer programmers, financiers or stockbrokers, and MBAs. Such stability doesn't come cheap. It has to be, once again, bred and nurtured over time. It's all part of the development of a corporate culture. Are your key people asked for long-range plans but paid for this year's ROI?

A well orchestrated, albeit lean, farm system for developing both the managing and doing talent vital to the future. Take a look at some of the leading companies with track records stretching back over the years, the records of GE, GM, TI, IBM, 3M, and so on. Most of them have evolved extensive internal programs for identifying, developing, and moving their more outstanding performers through the organization over time. There are multiple, qualified, enthusiastic, *trained* replacements for key openings in the company. There are people with the necessary strategic skills and personal characteristics who are available

---

*William G. Ouchi and Alfred M. Jaeger, "Type Z Organization: A Corporate Alternative to Village Life," *Stanford Business School Alumni Bulletin*, Fall 1977–1978, p. 13.

for assignment to build, hold, or harvest the different parts of the company as appropriate. And there always seems to be a small number of truly exceptional people who can be pulled up and plugged into unusual opportunities with high-risk and high-payoff potential.

Of course, having such a talent pool is theoretically easier in a larger company. What does an emerging company with a goal of keeping overhead cost down do? Its management stretches each key individual upward and outward. The president of one of the leading international companies in Switzerland never visits any of its twelve subsidiaries without taking along one of the nonofficer-managers. The CEO of a sparkling, younger Los Angeles company requires that each of his staff officers spend at least one day a month out of the office making contacts outside of his or her functional specialty. Each of six senior researchers in a fast growing Palo Alto chemical company are required to devote a minimum of six days a year to on-site customer visits at which no *existing* company business is discussed. These are examples of simple actions a senior manager can instigate to develop his or her human resource base without incurring the expense of duplication or of hiring expert human-relations staff help.

At some point in time, a growing company does reach a size where the simple and informal efforts of the president do need to be institutionalized. Internal management-development programs, manpower planning, career pathing, and individualized incentive systems all become candidates for organized attention and investment. The important danger to avoid is the smorgasbord approach in which too much human-resource enthusiasm leads to too many programs in too many flavors, with an end result of indigestion! The personnel farm system should support the strategic plan of the enterprise and be held strictly accountable for measurable results. If a reasonably direct linkage between the system and the plan cannot be readily identified and articulated, the farm system probably needs a critical look.

An entrepreneurial, "can-do" attitude that seems to acknowledge the temporary nature of today's products or services and market definitions, and to assume with confidence that necessary, informed risks should and can be taken to ensure the continued success of the enterprise. It is appropriate to close out this chapter on strategic management and the book on the high note of entrepreneurship—a term enjoying a resurgence of respectability and popularity after thirty years in near exile (1930–1960). For a long time entrepreneurs were only slightly more acceptable than outlaws. The go-go 1960s flushed out a new breed of business innovators, mostly with technical degrees, for the stock market investors to acclaim. The AC/DC 1970s in the U.S. sparked the notion that maybe entrepreneurship wasn't just the purview of the smaller company, that shifting resources from old opportunities into new ones is a continuing task for enterprises of all sizes. Now, in the 1980s, entrepreneurship is increasingly given front-cover prominence across the nation.

How does the alert management of an emerging company maintain entrepreneurship? Dividing and redividing the organization into discrete, manageable pieces helps. Publicly rewarding successful risk-takers helps. Variable compensation systems based on factors in addition to this year's ROI or EPS or ROS gives creditability to management intentions—and helps. But the actions and attitudes of a company's officers as they join with other key people to design and implement the company's strategic plans help the most.

Readings

I. Evolution and Revolution as Organizations Grow

II. Creativity by the Numbers

III. Norton Company: Strategic Planning for Diversified Operations

IV. Putting Excellence into Management

V. Corporate Culture: The Hard-To-Change Values that Spell Success or Failure

VI. Type Z Organization: A Corporate Alternative to Village Life

Reading I
Evolution and Revolution as Organizations Grow

Larry E. Greiner

A COMPANY'S PAST HAS CLUES FOR MANAGEMENT THAT ARE CRITICAL TO FUTURE SUCCESS

Foreword

This author maintains that growing organizations move through five distinguishable phases of development, each of which contains a relatively calm period of growth that ends with a management crisis. He argues, moreover, that since each phase is strongly influenced by the previous one, a management with a sense of its own organization's history can anticipate and prepare for the next developmental crisis. This article provides a prescription for appropriate management action in each of the five phases, and it shows how companies can turn organizational crises into opportunities for future growth.

Mr. Greiner is Associate Professor of Organizational Behavior at the Harvard Business School and is the author of several previous HBR articles on organization development.

A small research company chooses too complicated and formalized an or-

Author's note: This article is part of a continuing project on organization development with my colleague, Professor Louis B. Barnes, and sponsored by the Division of Research, Harvard Business School.

ganization structure for its young age and limited size. It flounders in rididity and bureaucracy for several years and is finally acquired by a larger company.

Key executives of a retail store chain hold on to an organization structure long after it has served its purpose, because their power is derived from this structure. The company eventually goes into bankruptcy.

A large bank disciplines a "rebellious" manager who is blamed for current control problems, when the underlying cause is centralized procedures that are holding back expansion into new markets. Many younger managers subsequently leave the bank, competition moves in, and profits are still declining.

The problems of these companies, like those of many others, are rooted more in past decisions than in present events or outside market dynamics. Historical forces do indeed shape the future growth of organizations. Yet management, in its haste to grow, often overlooks such critical developmental questions as: Where has our organization been? Where is it now? And what do the answers to these questions mean for where we are going? Instead, its gaze is fixed outward toward the environment and the future—as if more precise market projections will provide a new organizational identity.

Companies fail to see that many clues to their future success lie within their own organizations and their evolving states of development. Moreover, the inability of management to understand its organization development problems can result in a company becoming "frozen" in its present stage of evolution or, ultimately in failure, regardless of market opportunities.

My position in this article is that the future of an organization may be less determined by outside forces than it is by the organization's history. In stressing the force of history on an organization, I have drawn from the legacies of European psychologists (their thesis being that individual behavior is determined primarily by previous events and experiences, not by what lies ahead). Extending this analogy of individual development to the problems of organization development, I shall discuss a series of developmental phases through which growing companies tend to pass. But, first, let me provide two definitions:

1. The term *evolution* is used to describe prolonged periods of growth where no major upheaval occurs in organization practices.
2. The term *revolution* is used to describe those periods of substantial turmoil in organization life.

As a company progresses through developmental phases, each evolutionary period creates its own revolution. For instance, centralized practices eventually lead to demands for decentralization. Moreover, the nature of management's solution to each revolutionary period determines whether a company will move forward into its next stage of evolutionary growth. As I shall show later, there are at least five phases of organization development, each characterized by both an evolution and a revolution.

KEY FORCES IN DEVELOPMENT

During the past few years a small amount of research knowledge about the phases of organization development has been building. Some of this research is very quantitative, such as time-series analyses that reveal patterns of economic performance over time.[1] The majority of studies, however, are case-oriented and use company records and interviews to reconstruct a rich picture of corporate development.[2] Yet both types of research tend to be heavily empirical without attempting more generalized statements about the overall process of development.

A notable exception is the historical work of Alfred D. Chandler, Jr., in his book *Strategy and Structure*.[3] This study depicts four very broad and general phases in the lives of four large U.S. companies. It proposes that outside market opportunities determine the company's strategy, which in turn determines the company's organization structure. This thesis has a valid ring for the four companies examined by Chandler, largely because they developed in a time of explosive markets and technological advances. But more recent evidence suggests that organization structure may be less malleable than Chandler assumed; in fact, structure can play a critical role in influencing corporate strategy. It is this reverse emphasis on how organization structure affects future growth which is highlighted in the model presented in this article.

From an analysis of recent studies,[4] five key dimensions emerge as essential for building a model of organization development:

1. Age of the organization.
2. Size of the organization.
3. Stages of evolution.
4. Stages of revolution.
5. Growth rate of the industry.

I shall describe each of these elements separately, but first note their combined effect as illustrated in Exhibit I. Note especially how each dimension influences

---

[1]See, for example, William H. Starbuck, "Organizational Metamorphosis," in *Promising Research Directions*, edited by R. W. Millman and M.P. Hottenstein (Tempe, Arizona, Academy of Management, 1968), p. 113.

[2]See, for example, the *Grangesberg* case series, prepared by C. Roland Christensen and Bruce R. Scott, Case Clearing House, Harvard Business School.

[3]*Strategy and Structure: Chapters in the History of the American Industrial Enterprise* (Cambridge, Massachusetts, The M.I.T. Press, 1962).

[4]I have drawn on many sources for evidence: (a) numerous cases collected at the Harvard Business School; (b) *Organization Growth and Development*, edited by William H. Starbuck (Middlesex, England, Penguin Books. Ltd., 1971), where several studies are cited; and (c) articles published in journals, such as Lawrence E. Fouraker and John M. Stopford, "Organization Structure and the Multinational Strategy," *Administrative Science Quarterly*, Vol. 13, No. 1, 1968, p. 47; and Malcolm S. Salter, "Management Appraisal and Reward Systems," *Journal of Business Policy*, Vol. I, No. 4, 1971.

Exhibit I
MODEL OF ORGANIZATION DEVELOPMENT

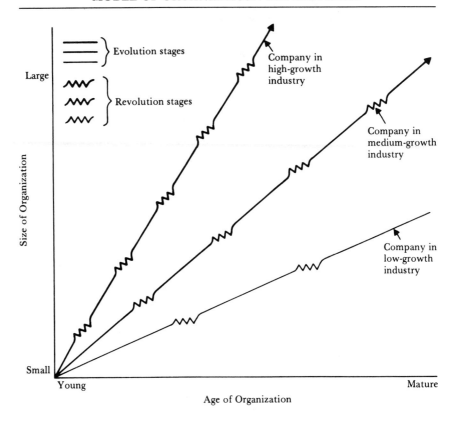

the other over time; when all five elements begin to interact, a more complete and dynamic picture of organizational growth emerges.

After describing these dimensions and their interconnections, I shall discuss each evolutionary/revolutionary phase of development and show (a) how each stage of evolution breeds its own revolution, and (b) how management solutions to each revolution determine the next stage of evolution.

AGE OF THE ORGANIZATION

The most obvious and essential dimension for any model of development is the life span of an organization (represented as the horizontal axis in Exhibit I). All historical studies gather data from various points in time and then make comparisons. From these observations, it is evident that the same organization practices are not maintained throughout a long time span. This makes a most basic point: management problems and principles are rooted in time. The concept of decentralization, for example, can have meaning for describing corporate practices at one time period but loses its descriptive power at another.

The passage of time also contributes to the institutionalization of managerial attitudes. As a result, employee behavior becomes not only more predictable but also more difficult to change when attitudes are outdated.

SIZE OF THE ORGANIZATION

This dimension is depicted as the vertical axis in Exhibit I. A company's problems and solutions tend to change markedly as the number of employees and sales volume increase. Thus, time is not the only determinant of structure; in fact, organizations that do not grow in size can retain many of the same management issues and practices over lengthy periods. In addition to increased size, however, problems of coordination and communication magnify, new functions emerge, levels in the management hierarchy multiply, and jobs become more interrelated.

STAGES OF EVOLUTION

As both age and size increase, another phenomenon becomes evident: the prolonged growth that I have termed the evolutionary period. Most growing organizations do not expand for two years and then retreat for one year; rather, those that survive a crisis usually enjoy four to eight years of continuous growth without a major economic setback or severe internal disruption. The term evolution seems appropriate for describing these quieter periods because only modest adjustments appear necessary for maintaining growth under the same overall pattern of management.

STAGES OF REVOLUTION

Smooth evolution is not inevitable; it cannot be assumed that organization growth is linear. *Fortune's* "500" list, for example, has had significant turnover during the last 50 years. Thus we find evidence from numerous case histories which reveals periods of substantial turbulence spaced between smoother periods of evolution.

I have termed these turbulent times the periods of revolution because they typically exhibit a serious upheaval of management practices. Traditional management practices, which were appropriate for a smaller size and earlier time, are brought under scrutiny by frustrated top managers and disillusioned lower-level managers. During such periods of crisis, a number of companies fail—those unable to abandon past practices and effect major organization changes are likely either to fold or to level off in their growth rates.

The critical task for management in each revolutionary period is to find a new set of organization practices that will become the basis for managing the next period of evolutionary growth. Interestingly enough, these new practices eventually sow their own seeds of decay and lead to another period of revolution. Companies therefore experience the irony of seeing a major solution in one time period become a major problem at a later date.

GROWTH RATE OF THE INDUSTRY

The speed at which an organization experiences phases of evolution and revolution is closely related to the market environment of its industry. For example, a company in a rapidly expanding market will have to add employees rapidly; hence, the need for new organization structures to accommodate large staff increases is accelerated. While evolutionary periods tend to be relatively short in fast-growing industries, much longer evolutionary periods occur in mature or slowly growing industries.

Evolution can also be prolonged, and revolutions delayed, when profits come easily. For instance, companies that make grievous errors in a rewarding industry can still look good on their profit and loss statements; thus they can avoid a change in management practices for a longer period. The aerospace industry in its infancy is an example. Yet revolutionary periods still occur, as one did in aerospace when profit opportunities began to dry up. Revolutions seem to be much more severe and difficult to resolve when the market environment is poor.

PHASES OF GROWTH

With the foregoing framework in mind, let us now examine in depth the five specific phases of evolution and revolution. As shown in Exhibit II, each evolutionary period is characterized by the dominant *management style* used to achieve growth, while each revolutionary period is characterized by the dominant *management problem* that must be solved before growth can continue. The patterns presented in Exhibit II seem to be typical for companies in industries with moderate growth over a long time period; companies in faster growing industries tend to experience all five phases more rapidly, while those in slower growing industries encounter only two or three phases over many years.

It is important to note that *each phase is both an effect of the previous phase and a cause for the next phase*. For example, the evolutionary management style in Phase 3 of the exhibit is "delegation," which grows out of, and becomes the solution to, demands for greater "autonomy" in the preceding Phase 2 revolution. The style of delegation used in Phase 3, however, eventually provokes a major revolutionary crisis that is characterized by attempts to regain control over the diversity created through increased delegation.

The principal implication of each phase is that management actions are narrowly prescribed if growth is to occur. For example, a company experiencing an autonomy crisis in Phase 2 cannot return to directive management for a solution—it must adopt a new style of delegation in order to move ahead.

Exhibit II
THE FIVE PHASES OF GROWTH

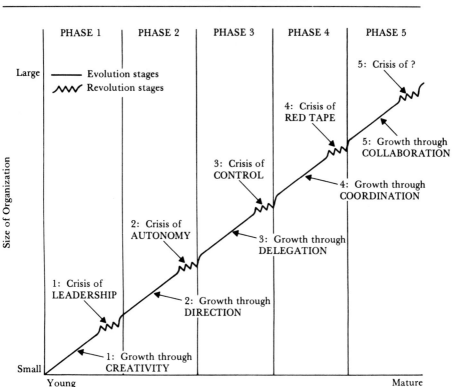

Phase 1: Creativity . . .

In the birth stage of an organization, the emphasis is on creating both a product and a market. Here are the characteristics of the period of creative evolution:

- The company's founders are usually technically or entrepreneurially oriented, and they disdain management activities; their physical and mental energies are absorbed entirely in making and selling a new product.
- Communication among employees is frequent and informal.
- Long hours of work are rewarded by modest salaries and the promise of ownership benefits.
- Control of activities comes from immediate marketplace feedback; the management acts as the customers react.

. . . & the leadership crisis. All of the foregoing individualistic and creative activities are essential for the company to get off the ground. But therein lies the problem. As the company grows, larger production runs require knowledge about the efficiencies of manufacturing. Increased numbers of employees cannot be managed exclusively through informal communication; new employees are not motivated by an intense dedication to the product or organization. Additional capital must be secured, and new accounting procedures are needed for financial control.

Thus the founders find themselves burdened with unwanted management responsibilities. So they long for the "good old days," still trying to act as they did in the past. And conflicts between the harried leaders grow more intense.

At this point a crisis of leadership occurs, which is the onset of the first revolution. Who is to lead the company out of confusion and solve the managerial problems confronting it? Quite obviously, a strong manager is needed who has the necessary knowledge and skill to introduce new business techniques. But this is easier said than done. The founders often hate to step aside even though they are probably temperamentally unsuited to be managers. So here is the first critical developmental choice—to locate and install a strong business manager who is acceptable to the founders and who can pull the organization together.

Phase 2: Direction . . .

Those companies that survive the first phase by installing a capable business manager usually embark on a period of sustained growth under able and directive leadership. Here are the characteristics of this evolutionary period:

- A functional organization structure is introduced to separate manufacturing from marketing activities, and job assignments become more specialized.
- Accounting systems for inventory and purchasing are introduced.
- Incentives, budgets, and work standards are adopted.
- Communication becomes more formal and impersonal as a hierarchy of titles and positions builds.
- The new manager and his key supervisors take most of the responsibility for instituting direction, while lower-level supervisors are treated more as functional specialists than as autonomous decision-making managers.

. . . & the autonomy crisis. Although the new directive techniques channel employee energy more efficiently into growth, they eventually become inappropriate for controlling a larger, more diverse and complex organization. Lower-level employees find themselves restricted by a cumbersome and centralized hierarchy. They have come to possess more direct knowledge about markets and machinery than do the leaders at the top; consequently, they feel torn between following procedures and taking initiative on their own.

Thus the second revolution is imminent as a crisis develops from demands for greater autonomy on the part of lower-level managers. The solution adopted by most companies is to move toward greater delegation. Yet it is difficult for top managers who were previously successful at being directive to give up responsibility. Moreover, lower-level managers are not accustomed to making decisions for themselves. As a result, numerous companies flounder during this revolutionary period, adhering to centralized methods while lower-level employees grow more disenchanted and leave the organization.

Phase 3: Delegation . . .

The next era of growth evolves from the successful application of a decentralized organization structure. It exhibits these characteristics:

- Much greater responsibility is given to the managers of plants and market territories.
- Profit centers and bonuses are used to stimulate motivation.
- The top executives at headquarters restrain themselves to managing by exception, based on periodic reports from the field.
- Management often concentrates on making new acquisitions which can be lined up beside other decentralized units.
- Communication from the top is infrequent, usually by correspondence, telephone, or brief visits to field locations.

The delegation stage proves useful for gaining expansion through heightened motivation at lower levels. Decentralized managers with greater authority and incentive are able to penetrate larger markets, respond faster to customers, and develop new products.

. . . & the control crisis. A serious problem eventually evolves, however, as top executives sense that they are losing control over a highly diversified field operation. Autonomous field managers prefer to run their own shows without coordinating plans, money, technology, and manpower with the rest of the organization. Freedom breeds a parochial attitude.

Hence, the Phase 3 revolution is under way when top management seeks to regain control over the total company. Some top managements attempt a return to centralized management, which usually fails because of the vast scope of operations. Those companies that move ahead find a new solution in the use of special coordination techniques.

Phase 4: Coordination . . .

During this phase, the evolutionary period is characterized by the use of formal systems for achieving greater coordination and by top executives taking responsibility for the initiation and administration of these new systems. For example:

- Decentralized units are merged into product groups.
- Formal planning procedures are established and intensively reviewed.
- Numerous staff personnel are hired and located at headquarters to initiate company-wide programs of control and review for line managers.
- Capital expenditures are carefully weighed and parceled out across the organization.
- Each product group is treated as an investment center where return on invested capital is an important criterion used in allocating funds.
- Certain technical functions, such as data processing, are centralized at headquarters, while daily operating decisions remain decentralized.
- Stock options and company-wide profit sharing are used to encourage identity with the firm as a whole.

All of these new coordination systems prove useful for achieving growth through more efficient allocation of a company's limited resources. They prompt field managers to look beyond the needs of their local units. While these managers still have much decision-making responsibility, they learn to justify their actions more carefully to a "watchdog" audience at headquarters.

. . . & the red-tape crisis. But a lack of confidence gradually builds between line and staff, and between headquarters and the field. The proliferation of systems and programs begins to exceed its utility; a red-tape crisis is created. Line managers, for example, increasingly resent heavy staff direction from those who are not familiar with local conditions. Staff people, on the other hand, complain about uncooperative and uninformed line managers. Together both groups criticize the bureaucratic paper system that has evolved. Procedures take precedence over problem solving, and innovation is dampened. In short, the organization has become too large and complex to be managed through formal programs and rigid systems. The Phase 4 revolution is under way.

Phase 5: Collaboration . . .

The last observable phase in previous studies emphasizes strong interpersonal collaboration in an attempt to overcome the red-tape crisis. Where Phase 4 was managed more through formal systems and procedures, Phase 5 emphasizes greater spontaneity in management action through teams and the skillful confrontation of interpersonal differences. Social control and self-discipline take over from formal control. This transition is especially difficult for those experts who created the old systems as well as for those line managers who relied on formal methods for answers.

The Phase 5 evolution, then, builds around a more flexible and behavioral approach to management. Here are its characteristics:

- The focus is on solving problems quickly through team action.
- Teams are combined across functions for task-group activity.

- Headquarters staff experts are reduced in number, reassigned, and combined in interdisciplinary teams to consult with, not to direct, field units.
- A matrix-type structure is frequently used to assemble the right teams for the appropriate problems.
- Previous formal systems are simplified and combined into single multipurpose systems.
- Conferences of key managers are held frequently to focus on major problem issues.
- Educational programs are utilized to train managers in behavioral skills for achieving better teamwork and conflict resolution.
- Real-time information systems are integrated into daily decision making.
- Economic rewards are geared more to team performance than to individual achievement.
- Experiments in new practices are encouraged throughout the organization.

. . . & the ? crisis. What will be the revolution in response to this stage of evolution? Many large U.S. companies are now in the Phase 5 evolutionary stage, so the answers are critical. While there is little clear evidence, I imagine the revolution will center around the "psychological saturation" of employees who grow emotionally and physically exhausted by the intensity of teamwork and the heavy pressure for innovative solutions.

My hunch is that the Phase 5 revolution will be solved through new structures and programs that allow employees to periodically rest, reflect, and revitalize themselves. We may even see companies with dual organization structures: a "habit" structure for getting the daily work done, and a "reflective" structure for stimulating perspective and personal enrichment. Employees could then move back and forth between the two structures as their energies are dissipated and refueled.

One European organization has implemented just such a structure. Five reflective groups have been established outside the regular structure for the purpose of continuously evaluating five task activities basic to the organization. They report directly to the managing director, although their reports are made public throughout the organization. Membership in each group includes all levels and functions, and employees are rotated through these groups on a six-month basis.

Other concrete examples now in practice include providing sabbaticals for employees, moving managers in and out of "hot spot" jobs, establishing a four-day workweek, assuring job security, building physical facilities for relaxation *during* the working day, making jobs more interchangeable, creating an extra team on the assembly line so that one team is always off for reeducation, and switching to longer vacations and more flexible working hours.

The Chinese practice of requiring executives to spend time periodically on lower-level jobs may also be worth a nonideological evaluation. For too long U.S. management has assumed that career progress should be equated with an upward path toward title, salary, and power. Could it be that some vice-presidents of marketing might just long for, and even benefit from, temporary duty in the field sales organization?

IMPLICATIONS OF HISTORY

Let me now summarize some important implications for practicing managers. First, the main features of this discussion are depicted in Exhibit III, which shows the specific management actions that characterize each growth phase. These actions are also the solutions which ended each preceding revolutionary period.

In one sense, I hope that many readers will react to my model by calling it obvious and natural for depicting the growth of an organization. To me this type of reaction is a useful test of the model's validity.

But at a more reflective level I imagine some of these reactions are more hindsight than foresight. Those experienced managers who have been through a developmental sequence can emphathize with it now, but how did they react when in the middle of a stage of evolution or revolution? They can probably recall the limits of their own developmental understanding at that time. Perhaps they resisted desirable changes or were even swept emotionally into a revolution without being able to propose constructive solutions. So let me offer some explicit guidelines for managers of growing organizations to keep in mind.

Know where you are in the developmental sequence.

Every organization and its component parts are at different stages of development. The task of top management is to be aware of these stages; otherwise, it may not recognize when the time for change has come, or it may act to impose the wrong solution.

Top leaders should be ready to work with the flow of the tide rather than against it; yet they should be cautious, since it is tempting to skip phases out of impatience. Each phase results in certain strengths and learning experiences in the organization that will be essential for success in subsequent phases. A child prodigy, for example, may be able to read like a teenager, but he cannot behave like one until he ages through a sequence of experiences.

I also doubt that managers can or should act to avoid revolutions. Rather, these periods of tension provide the pressure, ideas, and awareness that afford a platform for change and the introduction of new practices.

Recognize the limited range of solutions.

In each revolutionary stage it becomes evident that this stage can be ended only by certain specific solutions; moreover, these solutions are different from those which were applied to the problems of the preceding revolution. Too often it is tempting to choose solutions that were tried before, which makes it impossible for a new phase of growth to evolve.

Management must be prepared to dismantle current structures before the

Exhibit III
ORGANIZATION PRACTICES DURING EVOLUTION IN THE FIVE
PHASES OF GROWTH

Category	Phase 1	Phase 2	Phase 3	Phase 4	Phase 5
Management Focus	Make & sell	Efficiency of operations	Expansion of market	Consolidation of organization	Problem solving & innovation
Organization Structure	Informal	Centralized & functional	Decentralized & geographical	Line-staff & product groups	Matrix of teams
Top Management Style	Individualistic & entrepreneurial	Directive	Delegative	Watchdog	Participative
Control System	Market results	Standards & cost centers	Reports & profit centers	Plans & investment centers	Mutual goal setting
Management Reward Emphasis	Ownership	Salary & merit increases	Individual bonus	Profit sharing & stock options	Team bonus

revolutionary stage becomes too turbulent. Top managers, realizing that their own managerial styles are no longer appropriate, may even have to take themselves out of leadership positions. A good Phase 2 manager facing Phase 3 might be wise to find another Phase 2 organization that better fits his talents, either outside the company or with one of its newer subsidiaries.

Finally, evolution is not an automatic affair; it is a contest for survival. To move ahead, companies must consciously introduce planned structures that not only are solutions to a current crisis but also are fitted to the *next* phase of growth. This requires considerable self-awareness on the part of top management, as well as great interpersonal skill in persuading other managers that change is needed.

Realize that solutions breed new problems.

Managers often fail to realize that organizational solutions create problems for the future (i.e., a decision to delegate eventually causes a problem of control). Historical actions are very much determinants of what happens to the company at a much later date.

An awareness of this effect should help managers to evaluate company problems with greater historical understanding instead of "pinning the blame" on a current development. Better yet, managers should be in a position to *predict* future problems, and thereby to prepare solutions and coping strategies before a revolution gets out of hand.

A management that is aware of the problems ahead could well decide *not* to grow. Top managers may, for instance, prefer to retain the informal practices of a small company, knowing that this way of life is inherent in the organization's limited size, not in their congenial personalities. If they choose to grow they may do themselves out of a job and a way of life they enjoy.

And what about the managements of very large organizations? Can they find new solutions for continued phases of evolution? Or are they reaching a stage where the government will act to break them up because they are too large?

CONCLUDING NOTE

Clearly, there is still much to learn about processes of development in organizations. The phases outlined here are only five in number and are still only approximations. Researchers are just beginning to study the specific developmental problems of structure, control, rewards, and management style in different industries and in a variety of cultures.

One should not, however, wait for conclusive evidence before educating managers to think and act from a developmental perspective. The critical dimension of time has been missing for too long from our management theories and practices. The intriguing paradox is that by learning more about history we may do a better job in the future.

Reading II
Creativity
by the
Numbers

An interview with Robert N. Noyce

Intel measures "absolutely everything"–and
innovation flourishes.

In an inflationary era, the tiny computer on a chip that Intel makes is a dream product—as it becomes more efficient and more powerful, it becomes cheaper. With the cost falling by 30% a year, applications for microcomputers have cropped up everywhere, and the limits to their usefulness are nowhere in sight. Because of their small size and reliability, they have not only enhanced all the major functions of the computer but they have invaded the consumer market in digital watches and electronic games, to name only a few of their myriad uses.

It was at Intel Corporation, of Santa Clara, in the heart of California's "Silicon Valley," that the microprocessor, the specialized semiconductor chip that contains the "brain" of a computer, was invented in 1971. While maintaining its lead in the technology of microprocessors, Intel has developed more than 20 highly innovative products that have made the company an acknowledged leader in the semiconductor industry. By putting as much as 10% of all revenue into R&D every year, Intel has managed consistently to keep ahead of the competition with new products, and, as others have tried to catch up, it has enjoyed profit margins over 20%, twice those of the rest of the industry.

Intel's revenues increased each year from 1976 to 1978 by 43% compounded. In the next couple of years, it expects to reach $1 billion in sales.

Robert N. Noyce is vice-chairman of Intel. He attended Grinnell College, where he was elected to Phi Beta Kappa, and Massachusetts Institute of Technology, from which he received his Ph.D. in physics. He was on the research staff of the Shockley Semiconductor Laboratory, where he was involved in the design and development of silicon transistors. In 1959, with eight defectors from the Shockley Laboratory, he started a semiconductor division for Fairchild Camera and Instrument. While at Fairchild, as director of research, he helped develop the integrated circuit which was the precursor and prerequisite to the microprocessor. With Gordon Moore, another scientist-executive, Noyce left Fairchild in 1968 to start Intel. They were joined within a year by Andrew Grove, who had been associate director of research at Fairchild. Moore is now chairman and chief executive officer of Intel, and Grove is president and chief operating officer. President Carter presented the National Medal of Science to Noyce in January of this year for his work on semiconductor devices, especially on integrated circuits.

In this interview, conducted and edited by Lynn M. Salerno, assistant editor, HBR wanted to find out from Robert Noyce what it is like always to be the front runner in a fast-moving industry (it is "working on the edge of disaster"); his views on management of scientists ("they love to be measured"); and whether Intel experiments with flexible workweeks ("very hesitatingly"); about Intel's highly successful strategy ("we build on strength and try to stay out of competition where we're weak"). Finally, in a setting where even the president often wears a gold chain instead of a tie, Noyce described the environment as "confident, but not relaxed."

HBR: From its beginning, Intel has had a spectacular record. What's the secret of your success? Did you have a specific management philosophy from the start?

Robert N. Noyce: No, you didn't have to then. In a small organization there's enough communication so that the objectives are very clearly defined to begin with. If you can't communicate with only 25 people, your communication skills are pretty awful. So our organization was very sharply focused. We knew what product we were going after; everybody understood that very well. That was almost enough of a statement of objectives to last through the first couple of years.

What is the management style now?

Now we've run out of the collective experience of everyone. There's only one member of the board who has ever worked for a company larger than Intel— as Intel is today. And consequently, we feel that we're plowing new ground in terms of how we organize, how we do things, how we keep focus.

How do you keep focus?

Well, the thing that we've been concentrating on recently is the culture. What makes Intel *Intel?* A lot of it is what has evolved because of the personalities of the people around. It is MBO practiced all the way through. I think there's a lot of lip service given to MBO, and it's not practiced. But here everybody writes down what they are going to do and reviews how they did it, how they did against those objectives, not to management, but to a peer group *and* management. So that's also a communication mechanism between various groups, various divisions, et cetera.

Do you have a formal way to do that, then?

Yes, and it's pretty well built into the system. There is an openness, a willingness to discuss problems, identify them, which is not confrontational but rather, "Hey, I've got a problem. Here's how it's going." The executive staff, which basically consists of all the division managers, is truly an executive staff. They worry about the whole business, not just their own business, although they have the primary responsibility for their own business. There is very little in the way of staffers, as such. Staff work is done by line management as a secondary assignment. If we have a recruiting problem or a special project that needs to be done, we take a division general manager and say, "Okay, that's your secondary assignment for now."

How long have you had this kind of arrangement?

We just never have built a staff. We've always used line management for that kind of a function. I think that the way the business planning is done may be unique in terms of breaking the business into what we call strategic business segments. A committee is formed of the people, usually middle managers and below and a few senior managers, who make strategies, operate, identify trends, and identify the resources needed for operating that business segment. So that's a great training ground for oncoming management.

You don't have a separate planning function, then?

No, strategic planning is imbedded in the organization. It is one of the primary functions of line managers. They buy into the program; they carry it out. They're determining their own future, so I think the motivation for doing it well is high. Now that is not to say that we won't call on other resources. If we have a product area that we don't know much about, we certainly will call in a market research organization or whatever to give us more information to work on. But it is not a planning function that reports to the president, and it has no interaction with the organization.

Are there other important features of the culture?

The other essential aspect of the culture is that we expect people to work hard. We expect them to be here when they are committed to be here; we measure absolutely everything that we can in terms of performance.

Don't you find that approach difficult with the management of scientists?

I don't think it's difficult at all, because they're used to it. You know the old story about the scientist is that if you can't put a number to it, you don't know what the hell you're talking about. Well, as an example, customer service is poor—how poor? Let's measure what the response time is when a letter comes in, and we'll plot that versus time. Let's measure how many of the commitments on delivery schedules are met, how many are met in a week, how many are more than a month late.

What kind of people do you look for to work at Intel?

I think that the people we want to attract are, in general, high achievers. High achievers love to be measured, when you really come down to it, because otherwise they can't prove to themselves that they're achieving.

Or that anybody cares whether they are or not?

Yes, the fact that you are measuring them says that you do care. Then they're willing to work—they're not only willing but eager to work in that kind of environment. We've had people come in who have never had an honest review of their work. We get senior managers who come in, and we say, "Okay, in your six-month review, or your annual review, here are the things that you did poorly, here are the things you did well." A lot of these people have never heard that they ever did anything poorly. It's the new culture of our schools, you know, no grades. Everybody passes. We just don't happen to believe in that. We believe that people do want to be praised. So we try to do that.

That's an interesting outlook.

Even schools are beginning to move back to giving grades again. It was an aberration, I think, that occurred during the Vietnam War that was a very poor trend in our educational environment and was very poor training for people who wanted to go out into competitive society.

How do you keep making this a challenging place to work?

I think it's because people have the control of their own destiny, and they get measured on it. They get their M&M candies for every job, as one of our business instructors always said. It's now getting to be a real challenge because the billion-dollar company is clearly in view in the next year or so. The question is whether we can do it right. A great deal of effort goes into thinking about how we plan it, how we operate it, and how we build incentives into it. Where are we going? Are we going where we want to go? How do we win at this game called business? And, as I say, I think that our team is made of high achievers who really want to do that. They still see plenty of challenges.

Is there a lot of internal competition?

Well, there isn't the political infighting that you often see in companies. The direction is very carefully and definitely set, and everybody understands that. It's partly because of the way it's set—for both the MBO system and the strategic planning system. There just isn't any room for politics in the organization. It is very quickly rooted out. Someone who's crawling over someone else's body just doesn't get very far.

How does it get weeded out, though? The culture's strong enough?

No, I think the information is open enough so that what the individual manager is doing is put under a microscope once every six months by all his peers.

His peers know all those games, too, so politics just doesn't work. He doesn't get any support from his peers if he's doing that. It's an interactive company. Most of the divisions are heavily dependent on another organization that will let them get their job done.

You tried a three-day workweek some time back and that didn't work out. What is the situation today?

We still have a three-day week in Portland. If you have a capital-intensive activity, how many hours a week can you use it? What we do is run four 12-hour shifts on three days; so, 36 times 4 equals 144 hours a week, instead of three 40-hours, or 120 hours per week use of the equipment. It is simply a question of efficient use of the capital equipment.

So it wasn't a plan for trying a flexible workweek. Do you experiment with that kind of thing at all here?

Very hesitatingly. There are too many other parts of our society that are geared around the five-day week. The kids are in school five days a week. How does mama arrange to go to work? What happens to the family life if you take those work patterns and make them different from the rest of the family? In general, it doesn't work very well. It's sort of like a graveyard shift; there's a different group of people than on the day shift.

There seems to be a lot of control here. Is that a correct impression?

Oh, it's a very disciplined organization. *Very* disciplined. And we pride ourselves on our discipline. Did you see the little graph as you came in the door there, the Late List? It gives the percentage of people who come in after 8:10.

Doesn't that bother the people working here?

Yes, it bothers a lot of people. But they get used to it. And it becomes a point of pride after a while. It's another way of saying to people that they're valuable to us. How can we do our work if they're not here? Intel is the only place I've ever worked where an 8:oo a.m. meeting starts at 8:00 a.m.

Do you have any way for employees to get their gripes up the pipeline?

Well, initially, when the company was smaller, Gordon [Moore, Intel chairman] and I would have lunch every Thursday with a random group of employees. Now, that has broken down. You can't be very effective when you have 10,000 employees in the United States alone. Our total employment is over 15,000. But the lunch discussions are held at smaller group levels, and you'll find that if you walk around here at noon nearly every conference room has some sort of a lunch going on in it.

Are the employees expected to come?

No. Originally, my secretary would take an employee list and just invite the first 10 names and then the next 10 names, so it was alphabetical. Sometimes if we had a particular thing we wanted to probe, we'd take an interest group— people with common interests, all the personnel people, all of the college kids who had come in six months ago, or something like that—to get a different view on it. But usually it was a random selection. So if they were busy that day, they'd be invited next week, and so forth, down the list. We used to get through all employees in those days. They were invited at least twice a year. It did, I think, give you a sensitivity to what people were thinking out there. We heard a lot of bitches, and we got a lot of suggestions. We still do.

You have a rather spartan office. Is it typical of executive offices here?

Yes, I'd say so, for the older ones. The newer ones? There are none.

What do you have instead of offices?

The typical office landscaping sort of thing; no solid walls, open plan. Modular units that you can shift around as needed. In all the new buildings there are loads of conference rooms, so if you have to chew something you go in the conference rooms.

What if you have a private telephone call? Should you wait until lunchtime?

What kind of a private phone call would you have? I think that's part of the open communication. There are no secrets. I know the first time I started to think about it, it was shocking, but I had no hesitation to sit in any of those open offices and call nearly anyone. Occasionally I will use a conference room in one of the other buildings to make a phone call, but there really are just very few things when you stop to think about it that need to be handled that way. It's a habit to think that your phone calls are all confidential. But they aren't. Most people aren't interested. If the guy that's sitting next to you is somebody you trust and he overhears what you're saying, it doesn't matter very often.

Do most people like the open arrangement?

Yes, and there's a reason for it. We're social characters. Being locked in a box all day is not a very happy kind of situation when you get right down to it. Also, we try studiously to avoid the appurtenances of power. When we redo an office area we upgrade it a little bit. Part of it is an antisnob kind of a feeling.

Is there any kind of dress code?

You'll notice walking around here that less than 10% of the executives have a tie on. In fact, a lot of males here wear gold chains instead.

Was dress ever important here?

Yes. Ten years ago certainly I wouldn't have thought of coming into the office without a tie except on Saturday or Sunday or off hours, or something like that. It's much looser now. And if I'm not visiting somebody from outside the company, I will probably not wear a tie, probably not even wear a jacket. I will put on a sport shirt. It's sometimes shocking to people who come from the East Coast, although they're getting acclimated to it. They meet the president, and he's wearing a sport shirt and a gold chain.

Would you call this a relaxed atmosphere?

I don't think you could call it relaxed. A confident environment, but not a re-laxed one. One of the problems we have when people come in from other companies is that they just don't believe the intensity of Intel. They're not used to it. We're in an intensely competitive industry where change is very rapid, and there is no resting on your laurels because you'll get wiped out next year if you just sit back.

Doesn't that take an awful toll on people?

It does on some.

Do you have a company psychiatrist?

No, but we have lost some people. In particular, during both the recessions of 1971 and 1975, a lot of people left the industry and just never came back, feel-ing that it was not a relaxed place. But then we go back to the high achievers, the people who want to be where the action is. The crew is very young. The average age of the population around here is far younger than in the old es-tablished businesses, partially because Intel is only 12 years old. But also it's because we are very actively recruiting straight out of school.

When you started your bubble memory capacity, Intel Magnetics, you got three people who came from Hewlett-Packard to start it. Why did you do that instead of starting the project with people here?

It's a different technology. We had no particular expertise in it. We felt that the entrepreneurial start-up in a new field like that was the best way to get ivory tower types to focus on the real problem. That's an unfair characteriza-tion of those guys because they're certainly interested in the commercialization of bubble memories, but it was a separable entity that you could do on an en-trepreneurial basis. I think it's been effective.

You think that's a good way to expand your capabilities?

Oh, yes. It's a question whether it's related to your current activities. When it's not an evolution of your current activities I think it's extremely dangerous to do it that way. We try to keep the incentives, in terms of options and so forth, pretty consistent with the outside start-up and with people who are already here, so that it's equitable. And if the out-siders are enormously successful, they'll do better than the people here; if they are not as successful, people who are already here will do better, so it's a good incentive.

Do you try to find future markets by making the product yourself, or do you have people here who just study it without making it?

I'd say that in terms of the market areas that we're carving out, they're sort of the natural extension of the technology that we're doing. The only significant acquisition we've ever made was a Texas company, MRI, which is a software company. We did buy a watch company when digital watches were first coming along, but it was, in a sense, an entrepreneurial situation. It had 13 employees in it.

That didn't really work out?

It didn't work for us. We thought it was a technology game, and it turned out
to be a merchandising game. That's just not our game. What we're doing is
what we see as the logical next step of what we have to do. For instance, in
selling the microcomputer chips, we had to provide instrumentation to let the
designer design with those chips because it wasn't available somewhere else.
But that was an essential part of getting the microcomputer established in the
market. If we are going to do a good job of designing microcomputers, we
have to know more about software. So the software company was a major acquisition in terms of buying a capability that we didn't have, but that we saw as
a necessary layer of capability on top of the ones we already had.

**Are some companies dipping into your field so they can find out more about
your business?**

Sure, Hewlett-Packard is getting significantly into the semiconductor business.
Burroughs is, and so on. And it's important that they know more about this
business because it's an essential tool for them. It's also important that we know
more about their business because it's an essential market for us.

Are the lines starting to blur, moving up and also moving down?

Yes. Making semiconductors is becoming an essential technology to the computer industry, so they are participating in it. The computer is, you know, essentially where the semiconductor industry is going, so we're moving into some
fringes of their business. The technology is driving us there, simply because if
you're going to make ever more complex things, you are going to be making
computers. That's the major complex thing that is being built with the semiconductor. It might turn out to be a calculator or a controller for the tape recorder or the engine controller for an automobile, but it's still a computer in
one sense or another.

What's going to be the end of all this?

Oh, I don't know. I think it's that people do well what they do well, and they
succeed at what they do well.

There's not going to be a lot of bumping of heads?

There hasn't been particularly, no. The high-volume products are purchased
in the so-called merchant market for semiconductors. The highly specialized
ones, for which there is very little volume, have been made by computer companies for themselves because we wouldn't. We have no interest in making
them. Computer companies are not interested in manufacturing the design
aids to help build microcomputer systems, so we do that. You can define as
many businesses as there are companies in the business, because each has defined a different market that it's going after. Certainly IBM and DEC are both
in the computer business, but you don't think of them as the same. There's a

little segment where there's an area of competition, but in the main they're in different businesses. And I think that that's true here.

It's a good idea to know where your strength lies. Would you say that's one of the key things?

Yes, and certainly in strategic planning, the analysis of where our strengths and weaknesses lie is an essential part. We build on strength and try to stay out of competition where we're weak. Our strength is clearly in the components manufacture, in the design capabilities there, so that's where we want to compete. That's where we want to do battle with our competition. We certainly don't want to compete with IBM, anymore than we want to compete with General Motors. Just because we make an engine control, we don't want to make an automobile.

You don't want to be another IBM?

We'd like to be another IBM. I'd love to have 70% of the market. But getting into throwing rocks at each other is not nearly as productive as going on and building our own businesses.

When people like you and Kenneth Olsen and Edson deCastro, men who have been among the prime movers in electronics, are gone, do you think Intel and DEC and Data General will be different?

Hewlett-Packard hasn't changed a great deal with the changing of the guard over there, and I think it's because it was a well-conceived, well-built organization. IBM hasn't changed a great deal since Tom Watson left. If you think of the character of IBM now compared to 20 years ago, it's a little different, but you can't say that there were any major changes in the thrust of the business. And again I think it's because it was a well-conceived, well-executed management style that works, so there was no need to change it.

Would Intel change, then, without you and Grove and Moore?

I believe that Intel has been a very successful company, that we have innovated in terms of how things are done, in terms of management styles, and in terms of culture as well as products; and I think the momentum is there that will keep it moving in that direction.

How would you say Intel differs from other companies in your industry?

I used to characterize our business as compared to others in the industry as working on the edge of disaster. We are absolutely trying to do those things which nobody else could do from a technical point of view. We measure everything that we do so that when something goes wrong we have some idea of what it was that went wrong—a very complex process. We've tried to extend that same philosophy to the running of the whole organization. You don't do something unless you know what you're doing. You don't change something unless you know that it's been done on a pilot basis, that it won't louse up something else. And our industry's unique in that because it is very, very complex in terms of the technology that goes into it.

And it's very easy to make a mistake?

Very, very easy to make a mistake. We're working where a speck of dust ruins everything—that kind of an environment as far as the actual production is concerned.

You probably couldn't start an Intel today, could you?

I think you could start an Intel. It wouldn't be in this field. I think that there are still plenty of opportunities.

But it would take a tremendous amount of money, wouldn't it?

This field would. But there are significant companies that were started with relatively little. One of my favorites is called Apple Computer. And the guy started it by selling a car, and that was the capital. He started it in his garage, literally.

And he and his partner were only in their twenties, too, weren't they?

That's right. So it's like the start-up of Hewlett-Packard, which was done in a garage with $5,000. That was a lot more money when Hewlett and Packard started than when these guys started recently on $5,000. So, we're talking about those opportunities that are brain-intensive rather than capital-intensive.

But mergers and acquisitions are still cutting down the number of companies. How long will Apple Computer or a company like that be what it is today?

I don't know. A similar question is whether the acquisitions of the semiconductor companies have really decreased the number of competitors or not. They're still in business. Fairchild is still selling whether it's part of Schlumberger or not. Mostek will exist whether it's part of United Technologies Corporation or not. I was sad to see Fairchild merged quite as early as it was, in the sense that this last quarter we finally beat it in volume.

You weren't sad because of sentimental feeling about your beginnings there?

No. Just straight competition.

When you started Intel, did you have trouble getting capital?

No, we never really had any trouble getting money. It may shock a lot of people to find this out, but we never wrote a business plan, never wrote a prospectus. We just said, "We're going into business; would you like to support it?"

But you did have the experience and the expertise?

We had a track record. There was clearly a great demand for semiconductors. It was still a rapid growth environment during that time.

Howard Head once said that, when he started Head Ski, if there was a sales meeting to attend he'd attend it, if there was an ad to write he'd write it, if there was a floor to sweep he'd sweep it. That can be a problem for a lot of entrepreneurs. Did you ever have to do everything?

I've scrubbed the floors, I've done the glassblowing, I've run diffusion furnaces, and so on, in the past; I've done the customer calls and I've talked at sales meetings.

Did you ever feel that you had to?

No, those were the things to be done, so I did them. I guess if there is a frustration in a larger organization, it is that it takes longer to see the results of what you're doing. There's a massive inertia. So that you push on one thing and a year later you can see the movement. A small organization can turn on a dime and change direction. You suggest another way to do things and you can get it implemented in a week or two. When you have 10,000 people to change the direction of, it just doesn't happen that way. What you hope you do, or can do, is to break the organization down into small manageable units so that you can change the direction of one unit at a time. And I think that has been done effectively.

So being effective in the organization is the way you find a challenge?

There's an enormous satisfaction in seeing that you've really affected the society, and I have no doubt in my mind that Intel has really affected our society. If nothing else, the microcomputer revolution is an Intel-induced change that has occurred in our society. And we're just beginning to see some changes that are going on in the society because of it. It is much less necessary to be in the city for communicating now than it was 20 years ago. As a matter of fact, the necessity of going to work is much less now because you can have communication facilities at home so that you can work at home. We have several engineers who have their terminals at home. They can work just as well there as they can here.

In your role as vice-chairman, do you personally have more time to spend at home?

No. I intended to, but it doesn't work out that way.

How many hours a week do you work?

Oh, I usually get in here by 7:45 to 8:00 and usually go home about 6:00 or 6:30. I don't work weekends, at least, not in the office.

Do you take work home with you?

Reading. There are such voluminous amounts to try to get through to keep up with what's going on. I am willing to take more vacation time than I used to be able to.

Were you able to before but you just wouldn't?

Precisely. And actually that is one of the reasons why Intel was a two-headed monster when we started it. In the Fairchild situation, I simply felt that I couldn't leave and relax, which is a stupid way to run your life. One of the primary objectives in getting Intel going was to have it arranged so that I could leave and relax, and I started out with a partner that I could trust, whose judgment I trusted. Beyond that the energy goes into organizational building and team building, so that the team can carry on the job.

Now that you've removed yourself more or less from day-to-day operations, do you miss that?

Yes. How should I put this? I wanted to remove myself from the day-to-day operations so there would be more time to think about some other things, but that's a difficult thing to do, too. Some of the time you wonder about what you are doing. I mean, the complexity of the organization is such that it's an absolutely full-time job just to keep up with what is going on. It's several full-time jobs, as a matter of fact.

So it becomes dangerous to try to do something else as well as be involved in daily operations, because you don't have enough knowledge about what's going on and you make some horrible mistakes. Too many people depend on you to be right to take that risk. If you're going to try to do other things beyond that, then you'd better be sure that somebody is watching the store. But it is so habitual to watch the store that it becomes somewhat of a role crisis doing something else. I think that there are broader issues, however, that need to be thought about anyway.

Do you mean that there are broader national issues that you'd like to think about?

Maybe that's the motivation. Where's American capitalism going? Is it going down the tubes or is it going to survive? Where is the American standard of living going? Is it going to bread and circuses as it has been for the last decade or is it going to do what we did in the 1960s, that is, continually increase the standard of living for the population? Where's our international competitive situation going? Are we going to have the discipline to solve the energy problem in the United States? It's those kinds of questions that I think are important.

What is your major concern right now?

My major concern right now for all U.S. business is how we are going to compete with Japan. Because they're doing it right, and we're doing it wrong.

Well, we must be doing some things right. You are; this industry is.

But if you look at what gave Americans strength, it was the high level of motivation in innovation, the high availability of venture capital; and you look at the industry now, it's capital intensive. Now suddenly you have a major shift in the advantages and disadvantages.

What can be done about it?

As a nation we can't let Japan win this competitive battle because of complacency. I think we're much more alert to the situation than the automobile industry was—or the steel industry, the TV industry, the tape recorder industry, the ball-bearing industry, the bicycle industry, or the motorcycle industry. Just list them all as they disappear out of American society because of Japanese competition. It's a little frightening to think that this is happening in this industry right now. Yes, the semiconductor industry is healthy right now, but if we are to remain healthy, some changes will have to be made.

What kinds of changes are you thinking of?

In America, there's so little investment capital available that it's come to a situation where you pick the low hanging fruit and you don't worry about planting the new trees. You don't have the resources available to do both. And I think that's the thing that's likely to damage American industry. If there isn't a change in that, this industry, which is a centerpiece of American technology, could all be lost to the Japanese.

Reading III
Norton Company

Strategic planning
for diversified
business operations

Subject to the business-cycle swings of the capital goods industry, Norton Company experienced the usual drop in sales during the economic downturn of 1975. What was unusual for Norton was its ability on this occasion to sustain profits compared to the customary plunge in earnings whenever the economy dipped. Robert Cushman, President and Chief Executive Officer of Norton Company, saw this performance as evidence of the growing effectiveness of Norton's strategic planning.

As of 1976, five years' efforts had gone into developing planning activities that specifically could help top management shape strategies for the firm's diversified business operations. Mr. Cushman was pleased with the results of these efforts:

> *Our strategic planning has made a tremendous difference in the way the company is now managed. It gives us a much-needed handle to evaluate strategies for each of our many businesses.*

One of the difficult strategic planning decisions faced by top management in 1976 concerned a reevaluation of the long-term strategy for the coated abrasives business operations in the U.S. This situation is described following a

This case was prepared by Professor Francis Aguilar with the assistance of Norton Company to serve as a basis for class discussion rather than to illustrate either effective or ineffective handling of an administrative situation.
Copyright © 1976 by the President and Fellows of Harvard College. Reproduced by permission. This case was prepared by Professor Francis Aguilar.

general explanation of the strategic planning process at Norton Company and how it came to be.

The Company

Norton Company, headquartered in Worcester, Massachusetts, was a multinational industrial manufacturer with 85 plant locations in 21 countries. The firm employed almost 19,000 persons.

As the world's largest abrasives manufacturer, Norton produced both abrasive grain raw materials and finished products. The latter included such items as sandpaper and grinding wheels. The company also produced a wide range of other industrial products, including industrial ceramics, sealants, catalyst carriers and tower packings for the chemical process industries, engineered plastic components, tubing and related products for medical applications and for food processing, and industrial safety products. In 1975, these other products accounted for about 27% of the reported total sales of $548 million.[1] Exhibit 1 contains a five-year summary of financial results.

Organization

Norton Company was organized into "low growth" and "high growth" product groups. This organizational structure reflected two basic corporate objectives. The first was to remain the worldwide leader in abrasives. The second was to improve profitability through "a limited number of diversified product lines and without conglomeration."[2]

When introducing this structure in 1971, Cushman had remarked:

> As you look at Norton Company you see two major areas of business: our traditional abrasives products, which are good cash generators but have low growth, and our newer nonabrasive lines, which need cash but have a high growth potential. We need a different type of manager to run each business.[3]

Harry Duane, age 45, headed the abrasives group. His job was characterized as that of "running a large, cyclical-prone, slow-growth business with stiff competition in many different markets." Successful performance in this busi-

---

[1]On September 9, 1976, Norton Company announced an agreement in principle to merge with Christensen, Inc. for stock valued at $100 million. Christensen, with 1975 sales of $118 million and net income of $9.5 million, manufactured diamond drilling bits and coring bits for the petroleum and mining industries. With Christensen, nonabrasive products would account for about 40% of total sales.

[2]The *Norton Company Annual Report* for 1975 also highlighted three other corporate objectives: (1) to maintain responsible corporate citizenship ... which at times means accepting lower profits; (2) to maintain a superior employee working environment; (3) to enhance the value of Norton stock.

[3]*Business Week*, August 7, 1971.

Exhibit 1
NORTON COMPANY
FIVE-YEAR FINANCIAL SUMMARY
($ MILLION)

	1971	1972	1973	1974	1975
Net sales	346	374	475	558	548
Net income[1]	11.4	14.5	25.4	21.6	20.9
Net income, excluding effect of foreign currency exchange rate changes[1]	10.3	15.0	21.3	25.1	24.8
By Line of Business:					
Abrasives					
Sales (%)	70	75	75	75	73
Net income (%)	85	87	89	76	70
Diversified products					
Sales (%)	30	25	25	25	27
Net income (%)	15	13	11	24	30
By Subsidiaries Outside the USA:					
Sales (%)	41	41	42	45	49
Net income (%)	39	33	56	56	40
Working capital	148	151	155	159	200
Total debt	69	65	66	102	112
Shareholders equity	211	218	232	244	255
Operating & Financial Ratios					
Net income as % of sales	3.3	3.9	5.3	3.9	3.8
Net income as % of equity	5.4	6.7	10.9	8.8	8.2
Current ratio	3.7	3.6	2.9	2.3	3.3
% Total debt to equity	33	30	29	42	44
Per Share Statistics[2]					
Net income[1]	2.12	2.70	4.70	4.02	3.85
Net income, excluding effect of foreign currency exchange rate changes[1]	1.92	2.80	3.94	4.68	4.57
Dividends	1.50	1.50	1.50	1.575	1.70
Stock price (NYSE)	27–37	32–39	23–36	19–29	21–29

[1]Exchange gains and losses resulting from the translation of foreign currency financial statements were included for the first time in the 1975 annual report in determining net income in accordance with a new procedure recommended by the Financial Accounting Standards Board (FASB). The net income results, excluding foreign currency effects, conform to prior reporting practices at Norton and generally throughout industry.

[2]The average number of shares of common stock outstanding varied between 5.37 and 5.67 million during this period.

Source: Annual Reports and *Moody's Industrial Manual,* 1975.

ness was said to depend on careful cost control, keeping products up to date, and holding established markets. Duane had had experience in the abrasives business abroad as well as in the U.S. since joining Norton in 1957.

Donald R. Melville, age 50, headed Norton's diversified products business group. He had joined the company in 1967 as Vice President of Marketing after having served in various marketing capacities with Continental Can Company, Scott Paper Company, and Dunlop Tire & Rubber. As reported in *Business Week*:

> *Melville's management style relies on creating an entrepreneurial atmosphere . . . "In the case of abrasives," says Melville, "you compensate your people on the basis of whether or not they make that month's budget. In diversified products, you don't care as much about a month's budget—you try to double your sales in twelve months."*

The 1976 company organization structure is shown in Exhibit 2.

Concepts for Strategic Planning

In 1967, as Executive Vice President in charge of company-wide operations, Cushman faced the problem of assessing the role each of some 75 product lines was to play in Norton's future. The conventional corporate long-range planning then in use at Norton was found wanting for this task. Mr. Cushman consequently began to search for more appropriate ways to plan multibusiness operations. He later remarked:

> *During the early 60s, Peter Drucker, widely known spokesman, critic, and analyst to business began to describe business in terms of certain variables which seemed to determine a company's future. But it was Fred Borch, Marketing Vice President of the highly diversified General Electric, who in 1960 asked the key question and then assigned two members of his staff, Jack McKitterick and Dr. Sidney Schoeffler, to find the answer. "Why is it," he said, "that through the years some of our businesses fail while others succeed. There must be certain decisions, strategies, or factors which lead to certain results. With hundreds of products ranging from electric pencil sharpeners to diesel engines and nuclear plants, it is difficult to do an effective job of planning. It is, in fact, impossible for management to have a direct, personal feeling and knowledge about so many business environments. We need better guidelines."*

In 1967, Dr. Schoeffler was invited to Norton to describe the results of G.E.'s "profitability optimization" study. Based on sophisticated multiple regression analyses covering ten years' experience for 150 product lines at General Electric, Dr. Schoeffler had been able to identify some 37 factors which accounted for more than 80% of the variations in profit results. The findings showed how profitability varied with respect to such factors as market share, market growth rate, and the level of investments required. The findings also showed how profitability varied with respect to policies on such matters as

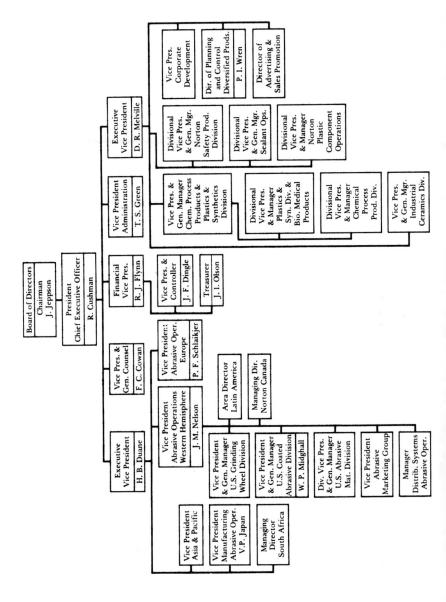

Exhibit 2
NORTON COMPANY
PARTIAL ORGANIZATION CHART, JUNE 1976

research and development as a per cent of sales, marketing expenditures, product quality, and pricing.[1] Mr. Cushman was struck with the relevance and concreteness of the resulting guidelines.

In his search for better guidelines, Mr. Cushman also became interested in the work of Bruce Henderson, founder and president of the Boston Consulting Group. Based on the premise that costs decreased with experience in a predictable manner, Henderson held that the firm with the greatest volume should have the lowest costs for a given product line. Market share served as a measure of relative volume for planning purposes.

The cash flows associated with growth and mature industries constituted a second element of Henderson's approach. Product lines with leading market shares in mature industries were generators of surplus cash; those in growth industries represented the potential cash generators for future years. For diversified business operations, Henderson urged that attention be given in strategic planning to the creation of a portfolio in which some product lines could generate sufficient cash throw-off to nourish the development and growth of other product lines in growing markets. Appendix A describes these ideas in some detail.

Strategic Planning at Norton*

The basic building block for planning continued to be the strategy analysis for individual product lines. This analysis considered a wide range of business factors such as competitive conditions, technology, and future trends, and concluded with a proposed course of action over time. Each strategy was prepared by the manager holding profit responsibility for the product line and was evaluated by group and corporate line management. The customary analysis and review of strategy was extended to include two additional tests based on the somewhat related sets of concepts described above.

One of these additional tests concerned the intrinsic profit potential for a business. Based on experiential data for a wide range of businesses (such as had been generated for General Electric), Norton was able to ascertain a measure of the profit level appropriate for a business as it existed. It was also able to ascertain the extent to which profits and cash flows might be increased under alternative strategies. These financial norms helped management to evaluate how well a business was being run and how much additional potential it had. Appendix B describes the kind of information available to Norton for this purpose.

A business strategy was also evaluated in the context of total corporate

---

[1] Examples of profit determinants would include: (1) high marketing expenditures damage profitability when product quality is low; (2) high R&D spending hurts profitability when market share is small but increases ROI when market share is high; (3) high marketing expenditures hurt ROI in investment-intensive businesses. The relationships were quantified as shown on page 155.

*All excerpts and material in Reading III that refer to PIMS and Dr. Sidney Shaeffler are used with the courtesy of the Strategic Planning Institute.

cash flows. The strategy had to conform to the overall availabilities of or needs for cash. For this purpose, market share performance served as a major controlling device. In broad terms, businesses were assigned the task of building, holding, or harvesting market share. "Building strategies" were based on active efforts to increase market share by means of new product introductions, added marketing programs, etc. Such strategies customarily called for cash inputs. "Holding strategies" were aimed at maintaining the existing level of market share. Net cash flows might be negative for rapidly growing markets and positive for slowly growing markets. "Harvesting strategies" sought to achieve earnings and cash flows by permitting market share to decline.

In line with this approach, Norton's operations had been divided into some 60 businesses whose characteristics were sufficiently different to warrant the development of individual business strategies. These subdivisions were know as substrategic business units. Combinations of these substrategic business units were grouped into about 30 strategic business units for purposes of top management review.

Strategy Guidance Committee

In April 1972, Cushman formed a top-management committee to assist in the evaluation of these business strategies. As Cushman later reported to the Norton Board:

> The function of the Strategy Guidance Committee is to review at appropriate levels the strategy of each business unit, to make certain it does fit corporate objectives, and to monitor how effectively its strategy is being carried out. It provides the executive, regional, and division manager an opportunity for an "outside" peer group to examine and advise.
>
> The committee totals twelve. The President, the Executive Vice President, the Regional Vice Presidents, the Financial Vice President, the Controller, the Vice President of Corporate Development, and Graham Wren as Secretary. Depending on the circumstances, business units are reviewed on a 2-year cycle. Well documented strategies along standard lines are sent to members for review before meetings.

Each strategic business unit was responsible for preparing a strategy book for review. Copies of this book were distributed to members of the Strategy Guidance Committee at least one week prior to the scheduled review. To focus attention on the critical issues, Cushman had set the following ground rules for the review session:

No formal presentation is required at the meeting because each committee member is expected to have thoroughly studied the strategy book.

Discussion during the meeting will generally center around these questions:

1. Questions of facts, trends, and assumptions, as presented in the strategy book.
2. Questions as to the appropriateness of the mission of the business, in terms of Build, Maintain, or Harvest.

3. Questions as to the appropriateness of the strategy in the context of the facts and mission.

4. Questions suggested by PIMS analysis.[1]

5. How does the business unit and its strategy fit and relate to similar businesses within Norton (e.g., coated abrasives Europe vs. coated abrasives worldwide)?

6. How does the business unit and its strategy fit within the corporate portfolio and strategy?

Involvement of Line Managers

The involvement of key line managers in the Strategy Guidance Committee and the methodology used in generating the strategy books gave a distinct line orientation to planning at Norton. Management for each business unit had to take a position concerning its mission, strengths and weaknesses, likely competitive developments, trends, and finally its strategy. The analysis and recommendations had to stand the test of critical evaluation by an experienced and involved top management.

Although Cushman was pleased with the planning tools Norton had developed, he felt that the deep involvement of line managers in both the formulation and review of strategies served to prevent a mechanical or otherwise undue reliance on the planning tools themselves. He believed it highly desirable that an operating manager's "gut feel" remain an important input to strategic planning.

Other Elements Related to Strategic Planning

In 1976 detailed cash flow models which could be used to support and extend the analysis described above were being completed. Several Norton managers remarked that these models would contribute importantly to the strategic planning efforts.

Also, Norton's incentive system was designed to motivate managers in carrying out their assigned strategic moves—whether to build, maintain, or harvest their business. Cushman reported the use of over 50 different custom-tailored plans for this purpose.

Finally, Cushman's deep-seated involvement in the strategic planning process and the respect he commanded from other senior-level managers at Norton undoubtedly influenced this process in major ways.

COATED ABRASIVES DOMESTIC[2]

One of the difficult cases for consideration by the Strategy Guidance Committee in 1976 concerned a reevaluation of the strategy to be followed for the U.S. coated abrasives business. Coated Abrasives Domestic (CAD), one of Norton's

---

[1]The acronym PIMS refers to the regression analysis described in Appendix B.
[2]Numbers for the remainder of the case are disguised.

larger operating divisions, had had a recent history of declining market share and profitability.

In 1974, Norton management had decided to stem further loss of market share by a major restructuring of the CAD division. During the ensuing two years, market share and profitability continued to decline. These unfavorable results raised important questions about the merits of the earlier decision. The case for holding market share (the current strategy) was further challenged by the recommendations resulting from the PIMS regression analysis. The PIMS report had concluded that the CAD business should be moderately harvested (market share permitted to decline) for its cash throw-off.

The remainder of this case presents excerpts from information presented to the Strategy Guidance Committee or otherwise known by its members concerning CAD.

The Abrasives Market

Abrasive finished products were generally classified as bonded or coated. Bonded abrasives were basic tools used in almost every industry where shaping, cutting, or finishing of materials was required. Some of the major uses were in foundries and steel mills for rough grinding of castings and surface conditioning of steel and alloys; in metal fabrication for such products as automobiles and household appliances; in tool and die shops; in the manufacture of bearings; and in the paper and pulp industry. Norton produced more than 250,000 types and sizes of grinding wheels and other bonded abrasive products.

Coated abrasives (popularly referred to as sandpaper) were widely used throughout the metalworking and woodworking industries, in tanneries, and in service industries such as floor surfacing and automobile refinishing. Norton produced more than 38,000 different items in the form of sheets, belts, rolls, discs and specialties. The most common form of coated abrasives was the endless belt, some major applications of which included the grinding and finishing of automobiles and appliance parts, the precision grinding and polishing of stainless and alloy steel, and the sanding of furniture, plywood, and particleboard.

The overlap of customers' requirements for bonded and coated abrasives varied from industry to industry. For example, the woodworking industry used coated abrasives almost exclusively. In contrast, the auto industry purchased large quantities of both bonded abrasives (e.g. for grinding engine parts) and coated abrasives (e.g. for finishing bodies). Industrial distributors, which accounted for a large portion of Norton's abrasive sales, usually carried both bonded and coated abrasive products. Both Norton and Carborundum offered full lines of bonded and coated abrasive products; 3M competed only in coated abrasives.

In management's opinion, the principal factors which contributed to a favorable market position in this industry included quality and reliability of product, completeness of product line, nonpatented technological "know-how," substantial capital investment, length of experience in the business, familiarity and reputation of name, strength of marketing network, technical service, delivery reliability, and price. In 1975, no single customer, including the United States Government, accounted for as much as 5% of Norton's net sales.

CAD in the Corporate Context

As was customary, the meeting of the Strategy Guidance Committee to review the CAD strategy was opened by Mr. Graham Wren, secretary of the committee, with a short presentation showing where the product line in question fit in the Norton portfolio of businesses. The first chart he presented contained an overview of the market share strategies for 31 strategic business units, as summarized in Figure 1 below.

Figure 1
SUMMARY OF MARKET SHARE STRATEGIES FOR THE NORTON PORTFOLIO OF BUSINESSES

Market Share Strategy	Sales ($ mill.)	Abrasive Operations	Diversified Products
Build	96	In the actual presentation, each strategic business	
Build/maintain	135	was listed under its appropriate category. For ex-	
Maintain	257	ample, CAD and 15 other business units were	
Maintain/harvest	60	listed in the abrasives column for the maintain	
Harvest	0	strategy.	
TOTAL	548	400	148

Separate charts showed the ranking of all business units with respect to return on net assets (RONA), return on sales (ROS), and asset turnover ratio for 1974, 1975, and the average for the two years. CAD placed in the ranking as follows:

COATED ABRASIVE DOMESTIC

	Rank Among 31	Value for 1974/75 Average	Norton Average, Operations
RONA	27	6.0	10
ROS	26	3.5	6
Asset turnover	23	1.7	1.9

A growth share matrix showed CAD to lie well in the undesirable low-growth/smaller-than-competitor quadrant (see Exhibit 3). As explained in Appendix A, a product experiencing both low growth and low market share

Exhibit 3
NORTON COMPANY
NORTON PORTFOLIO OF BUSINESSES ON GROWTH SHARE MATRIX
(BALLOON AREAS PROPORTIONAL TO SALES)

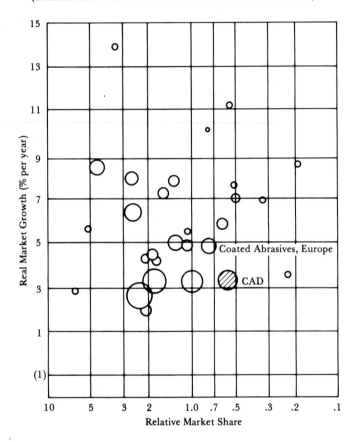

(relative to the industry leader) would likely be a net user of cash with little promise for future pay-off.

Finally, the committee's cash generation vs. market share corporate test was applied to the CAD proposed strategy. As shown in Figure 2, the combination of maintaining market share at its present level and generating cash was acceptable.

CAD STRATEGY PLAN

Paul Midghall, Vice President and General Manager for Norton's U.S. Coated Abrasives Division, was the principal architect of the strategic plan to maintain

Figure 2
THE CASH GENERATION/MARKET SHARE STRATEGY TEST

	Market Share Strategy		
Cash Generation	Build	Maintain	Harvest
Uses cash	A/?	U	U
Provides own cash	A/?	U	U
Disengages cash	A	(A)↘CAD	A

A = The combination is an acceptable strategy.
? = The combination is a questionable strategy.
U = The combination is an unacceptable strategy.

market share. His reasoning as laid out in the 1976 strategy book for CAD began with a statement of the division's role and strategy:

Mission—Cash Generation
   Norton's long-term objective is to allocate resources to high growth opportunities , while maintaining total world abrasives leadership. CAD's role within that corporate objective is: to be a long term cash generator; to act as the technical focal point for coated abrasives operations worldwide.

Strategy—Restructure and Maintain
   To meet that objective, CAD has in the last two years radically restructured its operations. Its strategy now is to complete the restructuring, to consolidate the organization into a confident, coherent team, and to pursue market segmentation based on the strengths which have emerged from restructuring. To understand how this strategy evolved, one must turn to CAD's history.

The strategy report went on to identify the reasons for the earlier deterioration of market share and profitability. These included

1. Inadequate reinvestment in the basic coated abrasives business in favor of investments which attempted to build allied businesses.[1]
2. High wage rates and fringe benefits coupled with low productivity and poor work conditions.
3. High overheads.
4. Premium pricing without compensating benefits to the customer.
5. A labor strike in 1966.

---

[1]According to Mr. Duane, coated abrasives and the other allied businesses had been organized in a single profit center at that time. The focus of attention had been on the total unit's overall performance. With the current approach to strategy analysis, each major product line was examined separately.

Serious attempts to reverse the negative trends for CAD had proved unsuccessful; and in late 1973, management decided a major change had to be
made to the business. The current strategy report reviewed the alternative
strategies that had been considered earlier:

> By late 1973, CAD's condition demanded positive action; share had dropped to
> 26% and RONA to 7.5%. A fundamental change had to occur. The principal op-
> tions were to
>
> 1. Sell, liquidate, or harvest. These alternatives were eliminated because: (a) a vi-
>   able coated abrasives business was deemed important to worldwide coated ab-
>   rasives business; (b) a viable coated abrasives business was judged important to
>   U.S. bonded abrasives business.
> 2. Attempt to regain lost share and with it volume to cover fixed expenses. In a
>   mature industry, with the major competitors financially secure and firmly en-
>   trenched, such a strategy was judged too expensive.
> 3. Greater price realization. We already maintained a high overall price level, and
>   3M was the price leader in the industry. In later 1974, Norton tried to lead
>   prices up dramatically to restore profitability but the rest of the industry did not
>   follow.
>
> Alternative—Comprehensive Cost Reduction
> A new cost structure was the only reasonable choice for a radical change. We had
> to scale down to a cost level consistent with our volume and our position in the
> industry.

In 1974, a decision to restructure the CAD business by making major cost
reductions was made by Norton's Executive Committee and approved by its
Board of Directors. This move was intended to make CAD more competitive
so that it could prevent further erosion of its market share.

Restructuring

The strategy review of 1974 had identified many areas for cost reduction.
These touched on almost every segment of operations and included the following: moving labor intensive manufacturing operations from New York to
Texas; combining the coated abrasives sales force with that for bonded abrasives (e.g., grinding wheels); and reducing fixed assets. The product line was
also to be reduced. Earlier about 4,000 product items out of some 20,000 (that
is, 20%) had accounted for 87% of sales.

During the two-year period of 1974–1975, over $2 million had been in-
vested to implement the restructuring. The changes were eventually expected
to result in over $9 million annual direct recurring savings, raising RONA by
about 8 percentage points to a total of 14%.[1] The number of employees for
CAD had declined from 2,000 to 1,300 by 1976.

---

[1] It was estimated that 3M had a RONA of 17% to 20% in coated abrasives.

CAD's Future Environment

The U.S. coated abrasives industry was expected to experience low growth and gradual changes as a rule. The strategy book forecasted long-term growth at 2.5% per annum. Industrial markets, which constituted 75% of Norton's CAD business, were to grow even more slowly. Because of the depressed level of business operations in early 1976, annual growth for industrial markets was forecast to spurt to about 7% until 1980.[1]

Product technology was expected to change slowly, but in important ways. The strategy book noted that

> *The advent of Norzon grain, new resin bonds, and synthetic backings illustrates the fact that although coated abrasives may be a mature product, it is not a commodity product. Technological evolution is slow but continuous, and a competitor who fails to keep abreast cannot survive.*
>
> *While product development exhibits highly visible evolution, process development is inconspicuous. No major changes have occurred, or are expected, in manufacturing technology.*
>
> *Capacity in all segments of manufacturing will be adequate to fill demand well into the 1980s.*

The U.S. coated abrasive market was said to have "healthy, strong, rational competition." With the exception of 3M, the return of most competitors was thought to be below the U.S. industrial average. Figure 3 [on the following page] shows sales and market shares for the principal competitors.

CAD Strategy for 1976

The proposed strategy for CAD contained two principal elements. One element was a continuation of the restructuring and cost cutting that had begun in 1974. CAD management estimated that about 75% of this program had been put into effect and that two more years would be required to complete the steps underway.

---

[1]An investment advisory report issued by Loeb Rhoades some months later (August 1976) had this to say about future prospects for the industry as a whole (bonded and coated products):

> *We have believed for some time that there were fair prospects for higher profitability in abrasives on a secular and not just a cyclical basis, merely because profitability had been poor for a long enough (seven to nine years) time. In a product that is basic to economic activity and that is capital intensive, and where no unusual reason can be discerned for the poor return on investment, such as foreign competition or technological change, etc., a lengthy period of poor profitability generally will lead to changes by industry factors designed to improve returns . . . At some point supply and demand come into a better balance, which then supports firmer pricing. And in fact . . . pricing had improved significantly since late 1974 despite declining demand in real terms.*

Figure 3
U.S. COATED ABRASIVES MARKET SHARE ESTIMATES

	1975 Sales ($ Million)	Total Market Share	
		1975	1973
3M	99	34%	32%
Norton	76	26%	27%
Carborundum	40	14%	15%
Armak	23	8%	8%
Other U.S.	35	12%	12%
Foreign	21	7%	7%
TOTAL INDUSTRY	294	100%	100%

Market Segment	Metal-working[1]	Wood-working	General Trade[2]
Market Potential, 1975 ($ million)	130	36	81
Estimated Market Share, 1975			
3M	30%	27%	65%
Norton	29%	26%	20%
Carborundum	22%	10%	11%

[1]Includes primary metals, fabricated metals, and transportation equipment (autos, aircraft) industries.
[2]Includes hardware retail and automobile finishing businesses.

The second element of the strategy was to focus on those market segments where Norton had competitive advantage. Detailed share/growth balloon charts, such as shown in Exhibit 4, were used to identify specific sectors for attention.

To foster product innovation, the 1976 plan had introduced a recommendation to expand R&D efforts. Twenty-two men had been assigned to CAD product development in 1975.

These strategic moves were predicted to produce favorable results. The CAD report identified the unit's future strengths to include: variable costs to be among the lowest in the industry; distribution channel relations to be among the best, especially with the close tie between coated and bonded abrasives; and a technological edge on new products (e.g., Norzon). The ultimate result, the report forecasted, was the generation of more than $7 million cash during 1977–1980. Excerpts from the summary of financial results are shown in Figure 4.

The PIMS Report[1]

The PIMS analysis for CAD had resulted in a recommendation at variance with that made by Mr. Midghall. A summary of these findings was included in

[1]As a subscriber to the services of the Strategic Planning Institute, Norton received on a regular basis analysis reports for several of its major businesses. These reports were circulated to divisional and corporate managers concerned with the business in question.

Exhibit 4
NORTON COMPANY
CAD GROWTH SHARE MATRICES
(BALLOON AREAS PROPORTIONAL TO NORTON'S SALES)

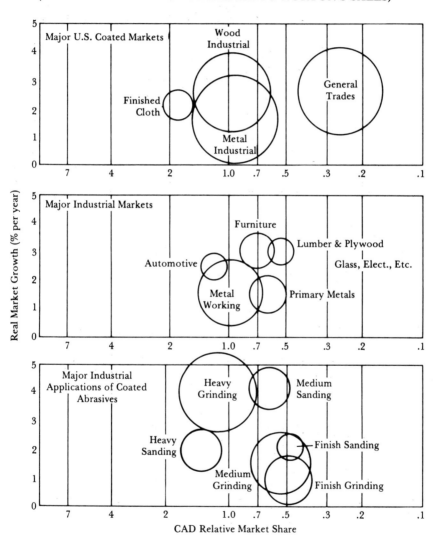

CAD Relative Market Share

Figure 4
SUMMARY OF FINANCIAL RESULTS
(NUMBERS DISGUISED)

	Actual						Expected*			
	1971	1972	1973	1974	1975	1976	1977	1978	1979	1980
a. Market share (%)	29.0	28.0	27.0	26.0	25.5	26.0	27.0	27.5	27.5	27.5
b. Net sales (index)	77.0	90.0	107.0	120.0	100.0	108.0	128.0	150.0	160.0	180.0
c. Net income (index)	215.0	220.0	310.0	230.0	100.0	140.0	480.0	760.0	810.0	950.0
d. % Return on sales $\left(\frac{c}{b}\right)$	4.7	4.7	4.4	4.0	3.0	2.7	4.6	7.0	7.0	7.0
e. % RONA	8.0	8.0	7.5	7.0	5.0	4.5	8.0	13.0	13.0	13.0
f. Funds generated ($ million)						(4.7)	0.5	2.5	3.4	1.3

*7% inflation per annum assumed.

the Strategy Book submitted to the Strategy Guidance Committee. The remainder of this section presents excerpts from the PIMS analysis:

The 1975 PAR report[1] indicates that the U.S. coated abrasive business is a below average business in a weak strategic position with a pretax *PAR-ROI of 12.0%. The business' operating performance has been very close to PAR with a 1973–75 average* pretax *actual ROI of 12.2%.*

The major factors impacting on PAR-ROI and their individual impacts are listed below.[2]

Major Negative Factors	Major Positive Factors
(1.5) Marketing only expense/sales	*1.8 Sales direct to end users*
(1.7) Capacity utilization	
(4.1) Effective use of investments	

During the three-year period, the marketing less sales force expenses/sales *ratio averaged 6% compared to the 4.1% PIMS average. PIMS findings acknowledge that high marketing expenses hurt profitability when relative product quality is low; i.e., it doesn't pay to market heavily a product with equivalent or inferior product quality. The average relative product quality for the business over the three years was estimated as follows: 10% superior, 75% equivalent, and 15% inferior.*

For the U.S. abrasive coated business, the positive impact indicates that selling through distributors instead of direct should lower customer service costs.

Whether the U.S. abrasive coated business objective is to optimize cash flow or ROI over the long term, the Strategy Sensitivity Report (SSR) suggests a moderate harvest *strategy. The SSR is based upon how other participating businesses with similar business characteristics have acted to achieve their objectives.*

The SSR suggests that the following strategy should be pursued to optimize either cash flow or ROI over the long term.

1. Prices—*Prices relative to competition should be maintained.*
2. Working capital/sales—*The SSR suggests that this ratio be lowered significantly to about 25% through primarily reduced inventory levels.*
3. Vertical integration—*Over the long term, the degree of vertical integration should be reduced.*
4. Fixed capital—*Don't add large segments of capacity, and maintain capacity utilization at the 80% level.*
5. R&D marketing expenses—*The SSR recommends that R&D expenditures should be reduced; and, consequently, the relative product quality remains in-*

---

[1]The PAR report specified the return on investment that was normal for a business, given the characteristics of its market, competition, technology, and cost structure.

[2]The figures represent the impact of that factor on PAR-ROI. For example, the higher marketing (excluding sales force) expenses/sales ratio noted in the following paragraph when comparing CAD to all PIMS businesses was said to have an effect of reducing the PAR-ROI by 1.5%. In contrast, by selling directly to the end users, PAR-ROI was increased by 1.8% compared to all PIMS businesses. See Appendix B for additional explanation of these data.

ferior. Also, the products should be marketed less energetically during the implementation phase.

The result from this strategy is (1) a gradual loss of market share from 26% to 21%; (2) an average ROI of 24% vs. the current PAR-ROI of 12%; and (3) a ten-year discounted cash flow value of $2.33 million.

A study was undertaken to compare the PAR-ROI of this business in its steady-state environment (after the recommended strategy has been implemented—1979–80) with the 1973–75 PAR-ROI. The results indicate that the strategy is successful in moving this business into a much better strategic position. The pretax PAR-ROI increases from 12% to 24%.

The major factors that had a significant impact on the improved PAR-ROI are Relative Pay Scale *and* Use of Investments. *These two factors account for a majority of the 12 percentage point increase in PAR-ROI.*

The general message from the SSR for the restructured *U.S. abrasive coated business is the same as for the* current *business, i.e., if the objective is to manage the business for cash flow or ROI, a* moderate harvest strategy *is recommended by PIMS.*

Management Considerations

Norton's top managers recognized how difficult it was for them to remain objective when deciding the fate of a core part of the company's traditional business. As Mr. John Nelson, Vice President Abrasive Operations Western Hemisphere, remarked:

> *There is no question that this decision has been an emotional one for me and probably for others, as well. It would be difficult to turn our backs on CAD. Yet, if the business cannot produce the target return on net assets, I think we are prepared to take the appropriate actions.*
>
> *I do not think that we are likely to close shop on U.S. coated abrasives. It is too important to other parts of our business to go that far. For example, Coated Abrasives [Domestic] strengthens our sales of bonded abrasives and is a plus to our distribution system in the U.S. It also provides us with a bigger base for R&D on coated abrasives. This benefits our overseas coated abrasive operations. Nonetheless, whether to stay with our earlier decision to maintain market share or to harvest the business was and still is very much at issue.*

Both Mr. Duane and Mr. Nelson remarked that the choice of strategy in 1973–1974 had been predicated on the belief that the industry could support a profitable number 2 and that Norton could play that role with its existing market share. The continued loss of market share was a cause of concern to them and to other members of the Strategy Guidance Committee. As noted in the minutes for the CAD review session of June 7, 1976:

> *In the shorter term period of late 1973 to the first quarter 1976, CAD market share dropped from 27% to 25%. Some of this drop was due to intentional deemphasis of the general trades segment. However, there was also an unintentional loss*

in the industrial segment. The key question is whether this short-term market share decline in the industrial area can be stopped and reversed.

The PIMS recommendations for an alternative strategy also served to raise questions about the soundness of the present approach. One Norton executive put in context the relative impact of PIMS with the following observation: "We are still learning how to use PIMS. At present, we consider it a useful input, among many, to our thinking. We would not reverse divisional management's position on the basis of PIMS alone."

Mr. Donald Melville, Executive Vice President, Diversified Products, made the following comment about the CAD issue:

> *You have to consider the dynamics of Norton's situation in 1976. We have done a lot to restructure the company, and the results in 1975—a bad recession year for abrasives—show our progress. But we are not yet in a position where we can harvest a major segment of our abrasives business, because that is the major guts of our company.*
>
> *By the early 80s our restructuring should be complete, and we will not be so dependent on abrasives. If we were faced with the decision in, say, 1982 instead of 1976, we could and probably should be willing to harvest CAD. In the meantime, we might as well repair CAD, because if we succeed, then we won't have to harvest it in the 80s. And if we fail, we will have lost very little.*

A relative newcomer to the top management ranks at Norton, Mr. Richard Flynn, Financial Vice President, made the following comments about Norton's approach to strategic planning[1]:

> *However the Strategy Guidance Committee finally decides on this matter, I think they are at least addressing the right issues, and that itself is something.*
>
> *The wide use of profit centers in large U.S. corporations has often led to bad analysis when different products were lumped together. Corporate-wide planning did not help the situation. Looking at a single product line family, as we are doing for U.S. coated abrasives, gives management much more meaningful data to work with.*
>
> *The other thing I like about Norton's strategic planning is that we are doing it repeatedly during the year. This means that we are always called on to think strategy. Looking at different businesses at different times enables us to take on different perspectives to our strategic thinking. This sometimes helps us to gain new insights for other businesses.*
>
> *All in all, the strategic planning sessions have been very effective in helping top management to think about and to deal with business strategies.*

Richard J. Flynn joined Norton Company in January 1974 as Financial Vice President and as member of the Board of Directors and the Executive Committee. He had been President of the Riley Stoker Corporation, a subsidiary of the Riley Company, manufacturers of steam-generating and fuel-burning equipment. He previously held executive positions with Ling-Temco Vought and Collins Radio.

APPENDIX A
NORTON COMPANY
The Experience Curve and Growth Share Matrix*

> "Costs of value added decline approximately 20
> to 30 percent in real terms each time accumu-
> lated experience is doubled."

This relationship, derived by the Boston Consulting Group from the study of many industries and labeled the Experience Curve[1], provided the basis for an approach to strategic planning for multiproduct companies.

The Experience Curve

The experience curve reflected actual, constant-money cash flows as opposed to costs from normal accrual accounting. The relationship, plotted on logarithmic coordinates, appeared as shown in the figure below. Such cost declines, however, would not occur automatically. They required good management and appropriate added investment.

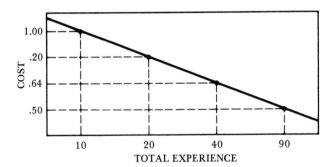

The decline in costs was thought to be the result of some combination of learning, specialization, improved methods, and increased scale. BCG pointed out the empirical nature of the relationship:

> *The experience curve cost effects are an observable fact. They can be confirmed by observation . . . Understanding of the underlying causes of the experience curve is*

---

*The material in Appendix A was based on information provided in the following brochures published by the Boston Consulting Group: "The Experience Curve—Reviewed," I through V, 1973, 1974; and "Growth and Financial Strategies, 1968, 1971."

[1]The name was selected to distinguish overall cost behavior from the well-known "learning curve" effect for labor costs.

still imperfect. The effect itself is beyond question. It is so universal that its absence is almost a warning of mismanagement or misunderstanding. Yet the basic mechanism that produces the experience curve effect is still to be adequately explained. (The same thing is true of gravitation.) . . . The principal problems encountered in application are those of defining cost elements and in defining the measuring unit of experience.

The experience curves for two distinctly different industries are shown below. Average price was used to reflect costs in these instances.

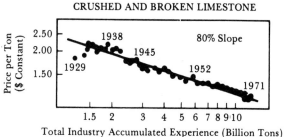

CRUSHED AND BROKEN LIMESTONE

Total Industry Accumulated Experience (Billion Tons)
Source: U.S. Bureau of Mines

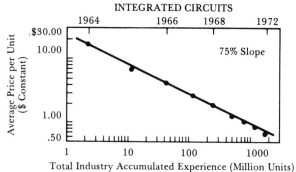

INTEGRATED CIRCUITS

Total Industry Accumulated Experience (Million Units)
Source: Published Data of Electronics Industry Association

Individual Firm Experiences

According to BCG, the experience curve cost decline for a specific product pertained to individual firms as well as to an industry as a whole. This premise led to an important strategic implication: for a specific product, the firm with the largest volume output should have important cost advantages over its competitors.

Market share proved to be a useful measure for relative volume and has become commonly employed for this purpose. For example, assume firm A is largest in its industry with twice the market share of firm B, its closest competitor. Then, following the 20% cost decline rule, A's costs of overhead and value added by manufacturing and marketing should be only about 80% of B's similar costs. Relative costs of value added as a function of relative market share are shown below:

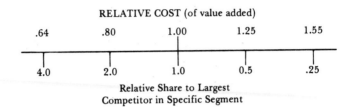

RELATIVE COST (of value added)

.64	.80	1.00	1.25	1.55
4.0	2.0	1.0	0.5	.25

Relative Share to Largest
Competitor in Specific Segment

The relative advantage for total costs would normally be lower than indicated above. Both A and B were likely to share in any cost savings (in constant dollar terms) resulting from supplies, raw materials, and equipment going down their own experience curves during the same time period. According to BCG, a two-to-one difference in market share would normally be expected to result in a five-to-ten-percent difference in total costs.

Growth Share Matrix

BCG focused on corporate cash flows as a critical dimension for strategic planning. Cost reductions associated with the experience curve represented a source or generator of cash for a firm. In contrast, investments associated with growth and expansion represented a use of cash. These two major factors influencing net cash flows were put together in the form of a matrix to highlight the characteristic cash flows for each combination of growth and market share. As shown in the figure below, the upper right-hand quadrant would contain businesses with a relatively low market share and consequently a relatively low cash inflow. These businesses would also be experiencing relatively rapid growth and a relatively high cash outflow.

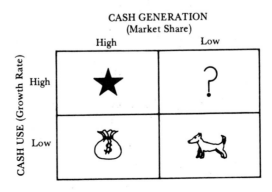

CASH GENERATION
(Market Share)

BCG had the following to say about the cash flow implications for businesses falling in each of the four quadrants in the matrix:

Stars are in the upper left quadrant. They grow rapidly and therefore they use large amounts of cash. However, since they are leaders, they also generate large amounts of cash. Normally, such products are about in balance in net cash flow. Over time all growth slows. Therefore, stars eventually become cash cows if they hold their market share. If they fail to hold market share, they become dogs.

Cash cows are in the lower left quadrant. Growth is slow and therefore cash use is low. However, market share is high and therefore comparative cash generation is also high. Cash cows pay the dividends, pay the interest on debt, and cover the corporate overhead.

Dogs are in the lower right quadrant. Both growth and share are low. Dogs often report a profit even though they are net cash users. They are essentially worthless. They are cash traps.

Question marks are the real cash traps and the real gambles. They are in the upper right quadrant. Their cash needs are great because of their growth. Yet, their cash generation is very low because their market share is low.

Left alone question marks are sure losers. They can require years of heavy cash investment. Yet, if they do not develop a leading market position before the growth slows, they become just big dogs.

Yet question marks are very difficult to convert into stars. Increase in market share compounds cash needs. The cost of acquiring market share doubly compounds cash needs. Question marks are sometimes big winners if backed to the limit. But most question marks are big losers.

Implications for Strategy

The growth-share matrix was viewed as particularly useful in dealing with multiple business operations. The concept of a portfolio of businesses was employed to plan corporate cash flows over time.

When the portfolio of businesses is introduced, it is by no means clear that all businesses should grow—even if they have the financial capacity to do so. Rather, all corporate assets should be viewed in terms of a balance between growth and liquidity, or cash generation versus cash use, with growth as a resultant. Viewed in this sense, every business within a corporation has a purpose, and that purpose is to generate cash or generate growth. Any business that does not fit this criterion is subject to divestment, and, in fact, should be divested.

The matrix, restated, then is as on p. 146.

The solid arrows indicate the movements of cash, with the broken lines indicating the desired movement of businesses over time.[1]

---

[1]The movement of businesses shown in the diagram cover two distinctly different approaches. One approach is to build a business from the wildcat quadrant (low market share) to a star position (high market share). This is typical of a "follower strategy." The second is to invest cash in research leading to products which will enter the matrix at the upper left-hand quadrant. This would be an "innovator strategy."

SHARE

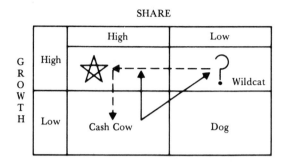

A growth share matrix for a company with multiple business operations is shown below. The size of each balloon is proportional to the sales volume of the product.

A TYPICAL SUCCESSFUL DIVERSIFIED COMPANY

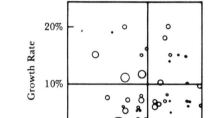

APPENDIX B

NORTON COMPANY

Profit Impact Regression Analysis

The Strategic Planning Institute was created in 1975 as a nonprofit, autonomous corporation to develop and to propagate a statistical approach to profit planning started in 1960 at General Electric.[1] Known as the PIMS Program (Profit Impact of Market Strategies), this approach employed a detailed multiple regression analysis of the profit experiences for many businesses. The resulting data were then processed to provide answers to the following questions based on the experiences of other businesses operating under similar conditions:

---

[1]The "profitability optimization" study had originated as an internal project of the General Electric Company, where it has been used for over a decade as a tool of corporate- and division-level planning. From 1972 to 1974, the PIMS Program was established as a developmental project at the Harvard Business School so that this study could be extended to a wide variety of businesses.

a) What profit rate is "normal" for a given business, considering its particular market, competitive position, technology, cost structure, etc.?

b) If the business continues on its *current track*, what will its future operating results be?

c) What *strategic changes* in the business have promise of improving these results?

d) Given a *specific* contemplated future strategy for the business, how will profitability or cash flow change, short term and long term?

The analysis to provide answers to these questions rested on the following premise:

> . . . that the profitability of a business is largely determined by general factors: growth rate of the market, market share of the business, the joint share of the company's three largest competitors, the degree of vertical integration, the working capital requirements per dollar of sales, the plant and equipment requirements per dollar of sales, relative product quality, and the like. Businesses with similar such characteristics tend to have similar profitability, regardless of differences in the name of the industry. Businesses differing in these characteristics have different profitability, regardless of similarity in the name of the industry.[1]

In 1976, several major reports were employed to analyze the profit performance for a specific business.[2] These included "Par" reports, Strategy Sensitivity reports, Optimum Strategy reports, and Cross Tables.

"Par" Report

The "Par" report specified the return on investment that was normal (or "par") for the business, given the characteristics of its market, competition, position, technology, and cost structure. It reported whether this business was the kind that normally earned 3% on investment or 30%, judging by the experiences of *other* businesses with *similar* characteristics. Also, it identified the major strengths and weaknesses of the particular business that accounted for the high or low "par" when compared to all businesses in the PIMS data base.[3]

Table 1 was employed to position a specific company business against the par.[4] The par reflected the pretax ROI that would be expected for the business unit in question (Business "12345"), given its specific characteristics. In this ex-

---

[1] The PIMS Program brochure.

[2] SPI provided three broad services to participating companies: (1) reports on the general principles of business strategy disclosed by the analysis of the data base; (2) specific reports on each business the company has contributed to the data base; (3) access to the computer models for strategy planning and simulation.

[3] The PIMS data base in 1976 consisted of information on the strategic experiences of over 600 businesses, covering a five-year period.

[4] The numbers contained in the tables were provided for illustration purposes only. They do not relate to the CAD situation in this case.

Table 1
NORTON COMPANY
PIMS "PAR" RETURN ON INVESTMENT (PRETAX) 1972–74

"Par" return on investment is an estimate of the pretax return on investment
(ROI) that in 1972–74 was normal for businesses facing market and industry
conditions equivalent to those of your business and occupying a similar market
position.

For Business No. 12345, Pretax

"Par" ROI	34.0%
Actual ROI	39.5%

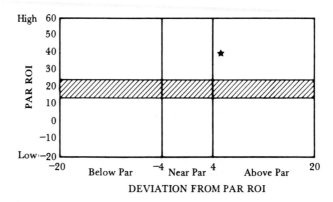

[The data on Tables 1 through 5 are for illustrative purposes only. They do not relate to
the CAD situation in this case.]

ample, Business 12345 should have earned 34.0% for the 1972–1974 period.
It actually earned 39.5%, placing it in the most favorable quadrant of performance—above par in a high return industry.

Table 2 was set out to show the impact of different factors, collected in
broad categories, leading to the difference between the par ROI for Business
12345 and that for the average of all businesses in the PIMS data bank. For
example, "differentiation of competitive positions" (item 3) was relatively favorable, accounting for a 4.1% of the total 17.3% that the pre-tax ROI for
Business 12345 exceeded "all PIMS businesses."

The broad categories in Table 2 were then broken out in more detail as
shown in the example below. (The normal two-page table has been omitted
from the case.) According to the data below, Business 12345 product price relative to competitors was such so as to lessen ROI by 1.2% compared to all
PIMS businesses. The relative pay scale for Business 12345, however, had a
3.9% favorable impact on ROI. The combined impact of the five factors to-
taled the 4.1% found in Table 2.

Table 2
NORTON COMPANY
PIMS IMPACT ON "PAR" ROI OF THE FACTORS BY CATEGORY

"Par" ROI equals the sum of the total impact and the average ROI of all businesses in the PIMS data base.

Category	Impact on "Par" ROI (Pretax) %
Attractiveness of business environment	0.6
Strength of your competitive position	1.9
Differentiation of competitive position	4.1
Effectiveness of use of investment	4.5
Discretionary budget allocation	5.4
Company factors	0.2
Change/Action factors	0.5
Total Impact	17.3
Average ROI, All PIMS Businesses	16.7
"PAR" ROI, Business 12345	34.0%

Factors	Impact of Factor on PAR ROI (%)
Differentiation of Competitive Position	4.1%
Price relative to competition	−1.2
Relative pay scale	3.9
Product quality	1.3
New product sales (% total sales)	−0.8
Manufacturing costs/sales	0.9

Strategy Sensitivity Report

This report indicated the short- and long-term changes in profit likely to occur based on specific strategic moves which might be employed. The output reflected the experiences of other businesses making a similar move, from a similar starting point, in a similar business environment.

The analysis required as input a number of key assumptions concerning the future environment. These are shown at the top of Table 3 for Business 12345. The bottom of Table 3 shows various results for profits and ROI associated with specific decisions concerning market share. For example, discounted net income for a ten-year period would increase with market share. The opposite would be true for discounted cash flow in this illustration.

The data for each of the market share strategies was elaborated in a subsequent table. Table 4 shows such data for the strategy of a major increase in market share. Data comparable to that shown in Tables 4 and 5 were also provided for strategic variables other than market share, such as decisions concerning vertical integration and investment intensity. Additional tables could

Table 3
NORTON COMPANY
PIMS STRATEGY SENSITIVITY REPORT
SUMMARY

"MOST LIKELY" ENVIRONMENT
KEY ASSUMPTIONS: BUSINESS 12345

	1975-78	1978-84
INDUSTRY SALES GROWTH RATE	7.5%	5.6%
ANNUAL CHANGE IN SELLING PRICE	4.4%	5.2%
ANNUAL CHANGE IN WAGE RATES	5.1%	
ANNUAL CHANGE IN MATERIAL COST	5.1%	
ANNUAL CHANGE IN PLANT COST	8.0%	6.0%

TIME DISCOUNT RATE	8.0%
CAPITAL CHARGE RATE	6.0%
TAX RATE	50.0%
DIVIDEND PAYOUT RATE	0.0%

"QUANTUM" OF ADDITIONAL CAPACITY	2.0%
TARGETED CAPACITY UTILIZATION	80.0%
ANNUAL DEPRECIATION RATE	12.0%

DEVIATIONS FROM:	ACTUAL HISTORICAL	ASSUMED FUTURE
PAR ROI	5.5	5.5
DELTA ROI	1.4	0.0

M A R K E T   S H A R E

	DECREASE		NO PLANNED	INCREASE	
SUMMARY RESULTS OF:	MAJOR	SMALL	CHANGE	SMALL	MAJOR
MARKET SHARE 1979	16.	20.	23.	27.	31.
NET SALES BILLED 1979	1144.	1364.	1603.	1863.	2147.
NET INCOME 1979	91.	103.	126.	151.	182.
AVERAGE INVESTMENT 1979	221.	240.	290.	343.	399.
ROI 1977 (%)	58.	49.	40.	30.	20.
ROI 1979 (%)	41.	43.	43.	44.	45.
ROI 1984 (%)	42.	43.	44.	45.	47.
DISCOUNTD NET INCOME 10YR	737.	763.	812.	853.	898.
DISCOUNTED CASH FLOW 10YR	373.	364.	360.	353.	348.
DISC CSH FLW + INVST 10YR	236.	245.	260.	271.	284.
COMBINED INCOME 10YR	405.	426.	454.	474.	496.
AVERAGE NET INCOME 3YR	120.	112.	105.	95.	80.
DISC CSH FL YLD RATE 10YR (%)	23.	22.	21.	20.	19.
AVERAGE ROI 5YR (%)	49.	45.	41.	36.	32.
INDEX OF NET INC CHNG 5YR (%)	-1.	0.	2.	3.	5.

INCREMENTAL RETURN ON INCREASED INVESTMENT FOR MORE AMBITIOUS STRATEGY :
    DISCOUNTD NET INCOME (SMALL INCR - SMALL DECR) =   90.
    90. / INVSTMNT 1979 (SMALL INCR - SMALL DECR) =   89.%

Table 4
NORTON COMPANY
PIMS STRATEGY SENSITIVITY REPORT
DETAILS: BUSINESS 12345

STRATEGY MOVE: MAJOR INCREASE IN MARKET SHARE

	RECENT POSITION (1972-74)	DURING STRATEGY IMPLEMENTATION (1977)	NEW STEADY-STATE POSITION (1979)	NEW LONG-TERM POSITION (1984)
NET SALES (CURRENT$)	1102.4	1609.3	2146.8	2819.1
NET INCOME	102.6	68.0	181.6	198.2
AVERAGE INVESTMENT	259.5	336.1	399.3	421.1
NET CASH FLOW	43.8	8.5	59.2	94.7
RETURN ON INVESTMENT	39.5%	20.2%	45.5%	47.1%
RETURN ON SALES	9.3%	4.2%	8.5%	7.0%
FACTORS				
COMPETITIVE POSITION:				
MARKET SHARE	22.3	26.2	30.8	30.8
RELATIVE MARKET SHARE	51.9	64.3	80.5	80.5
RELATIVE PRICE INDEX	3.0	3.0	3.0	3.0
PRODUCT QUALITY	60.3	68.9	65.2	65.2
USE OF INVESTMENT:				
INVESTMENT/VALUE ADDED	50.8	44.1	40.0	31.9
INVESTMENT/SALES	23.5	20.9	18.6	14.9
FIXED CAPITAL INTENSITY	20.7	17.6	17.4	15.2
NET BOOK/GROSS BOOK VALUE	55.1	46.3	48.5	31.6
VALUE ADDED/SALES	48.6	48.4	48.6	48.6
WORKING CAPITAL/SALES	12.1	12.7	10.1	10.1
CAPACITY UTILIZATION	74.0	79.4	78.6	79.8
SALES/EMPLOYEES	55750.	55517.	57028.	57652.
BUDGET ALLOCATIONS:				
MARKETING EXPENSES/SALES	7.8	8.6	7.4	7.4
R+D EXPENSES/SALES	2.6	3.7	2.8	2.8

PERFORMANCE MEASURES:

DISCOUNTED NET INCOME 10YR	898.1
DISCOUNTED CASH FLOW 10YR	348.2
DISCOUNTD CASH FLOW + INVSTMENT 10YR	283.7
COMBINED INCOME 10YR	495.6
AVERAGE NET INCOME 3YR	79.5
DISCOUNTED CASH FLOW YIELD RATE 10YR	19.2%
AVERAGE RETURN ON INVESTMENT 5YR	32.1%
INDEX OF NET INCOME CHANGE 5YR	4.7%

Table 5
NORTON COMPANY
PIMS STRATEGY SENSITIVITY REPORT
DETAILS: BUSINESS 12345

STRATEGY: TO OPTIMIZE
DISCOUNTED CASH FLOW 10YR

	RECENT POSITION (1972-74)	DURING STRATEGY IMPLEMENTATION (1977)	NEW STEADY-STATE POSITION (1979)	NEW LONG-TERM POSITION (1984)
NET SALES (CURRENT$)	1102.4	1142.2	1081.4	1420.0
NET INCOME	102.6	128.4	86.4	108.0
AVERAGE INVESTMENT	259.5	227.5	203.7	247.9
NET CASH FLOW	43.8	74.8	55.1	45.2
RETURN ON INVESTMENT	39.5%	56.4%	42.4%	43.6%
RETURN ON SALES	9.3%	11.2%	8.0%	7.6%

F A C T O R S

COMPETITIVE POSITION:				
MARKET SHARE	22.3	18.6	15.5	15.5
RELATIVE MARKET SHARE	51.9	41.3	33.2	33.2
RELATIVE PRICE INDEX	3.0	2.9	3.0	3.0
PRODUCT QUALITY	60.3	49.0	56.4	56.4
USE OF INVESTMENT:				
INVESTMENT/VALUE ADDED	50.8	40.1	35.2	32.6
INVESTMENT/SALES	23.5	19.9	18.8	17.5
FIXED CAPITAL INTENSITY	20.7	16.5	14.3	14.1
NET BOOK/GROSS BOOK VALUE	55.1	45.6	43.0	34.0
VALUE ADDED/SALES	48.6	52.6	55.7	55.7
WORKING CAPITAL/SALES	12.1	12.4	12.7	12.7
CAPACITY UTILIZATION	74.0	80.0	80.0	80.0
SALES/EMPLOYEES	55750.	47536.	44461.	47667.
BUDGET ALLOCATIONS:				
MARKETING EXPENSES/SALES	7.8	7.2	8.1	8.1
R+D EXPENSES/SALES	2.6	1.6	2.7	2.7

P E R F O R M A N C E   M E A S U R E S :

DISCOUNTED NET INCOME 10YR	725.9
DISCOUNTED CASH FLOW 10YR	377.1
DISCOUNTD CASH FLOW + INVSTMENT 10YR	232.4
COMBINED INCOME 10YR	404.0
AVERAGE NET INCOME 3YR	119.8
DISCOUNTED CASH FLOW YIELD RATE 10YR	23.1%
AVERAGE RETURN ON INVESTMENT 5YR	48.8%
INDEX OF NET INCOME CHANGE 5YR	-1.4%

also be prepared which recast the data with selected changes in the original assumptions—for example, higher inflation, a recession, higher interest rates, etc.

Optimum Strategy Report

This report indicated that combination of several strategic moves that promised to give optimal results for the business, judging by the experiences of other businesses under similar circumstances. Table 5 shows the strategy to be followed in terms of 14 factors in order to maximize discounted cash flow over a ten-year period. Similar tables were prepared to show the strategies to optimize discounted net income for 10 years, average ROI for five years, and average net income for three years.

Cross Tables

To provide further guidance for changing specific elements of a strategy, data were provided to show the effects on ROI by varying one business factor versus another. The figure below illustrates the cross table for marketing expenditures as a percent of sales versus product quality. Inspection of these data shows that relatively high marketing expenditures were counter-productive when product quality was relatively low (ROI decreased from 15% to 3%). Cross tables were available for other factor combinations such as:[1]

> R&D costs/Sales vs. Investment/Sales
> Product quality vs. Relative market share
> Marketing costs excluding sales force/Sales vs. Investment/Sales
> Inventory/Sales vs. Fixed capital intensity

		Marketing Costs/Sales Revenues		
		Low	Medium	High
Product Quality	Low	15	15	3
	Medium	18	17	14
	High	25$_x$	26	20

Number in each box is the average pretax ROI for all PIMS businesses in that box.
The x marks the location of Business 12345.

---

[1]For further information about the use of cross tables and PIMS in general, see: "Impact of Strategic Planning on Profit Performance," *Harvard Business Review*, March-April 1974; and "Market Share—A Key to Profitability, "*Harvard Business Review*, January-February 1975.

Reading IV
Putting Excellence into Management

Thomas J. Peters

What makes for excellence in the management of a company? Is it the use of sophisticated management techniques such as zero-based budgeting, management by objectives, matrix organization, and sector, group, or portfolio management? Is it greater use of computers to control companies that continue to grow even larger in size and more diverse in activities? Is it a battalion of specialized MBAs, well-versed in the techniques of strategic planning?

Probably not. Although most well-run companies use a fair sampling of all these tools, they do not use them as substitutes for the basics of good management. Indeed, McKinsey & Co., a management consultant concern, has studied management practices at 37 companies that are often used as examples of well-run organizations and has found that they have eight common attributes. None of those attributes depends on "modern" management tools or gimmicks. In fact, none of them requires high technology, and none of them costs a cent to implement. All that is needed is time, energy, and a willingness on the part of management to think rather than to make use of management formulas.

The outstanding performers work hard to keep things simple. They rely on simple organizational structures, simple strategies, simple goals, and simple communications. The eight attributes that characterize their managements are

Thomas J. Peters is a principal in McKinsey & Co., where he is co-leader of organization effectiveness practice. He also teaches at Stanford University Graduate School of Business.

- A bias toward action.
- Simple form and lean staff.
- Continued contact with customers.
- Productivity improvement via people.
- Operational autonomy to encourage entrepreneurship.
- Stress on one key business value.
- Emphasis on doing what they know best.
- Simultaneous loose-tight controls.

Although none of these sounds startling or new, most are conspicuously absent in many companies today. Far too many managers have lost sight of the basics—service to customers, low-cost manufacturing, productivity improvement, innovation, and risk-taking. In many cases, they have been seduced by the availability of MBAs, armed with the "latest" in strategic planning techniques. MBAs who specialize in strategy are bright, but they often cannot implement their ideas, and their companies wind up losing the capacity to act. At Standard Brands Inc., for example, Chairman F. Ross Johnson discovered this the hard way when he brought a handful of planning specialists into his consumer products company. "The guys who were bright [the strategic planners] were not the kinds of people who could implement programs," he lamented to Business Week. Two years later, he removed the planners.

Another consumer products company followed a similar route, hiring a large band of young MBAs for the staffs of senior vice-presidents. The new people were assigned to build computer models for designing new products. Yet none of the products could be manufactured or brought to market. Complained one line executive: "The models incorporated 83 variables in product planning, but we were being killed by just one—cost."

Companies are being stymied not only by their own staffs but often by their structure. McKinsey studied one company where the new-product process required 223 separate committees to approve an idea before it could be put into production. Another company was restructured recently into 200 strategic business units—only to discover that it was impossible to implement 200 strategies. And even at General Electric Co., which is usually cited for its ability to structure itself according to its management needs, an executive recently complained: "Things become bureaucratic with astonishing speed. Inevitably when we wire things up, we lose vitality." Emerson Electric Co., with a much simpler structure than GE, consistently beats its huge competitor on costs—manufacturing its products in plants with fewer than 600 employees.

McKinsey's study focused on 10 well-managed companies: International Business Machines, Texas Instruments, Hewlett-Packard, 3M, Digital Equipment, Procter & Gamble, Johnson & Johnson, McDonald's, Dana, and Emerson Electric. On the surface, they have nothing in common. There is no universality of product line: Five are in high technology; one is in packaged goods; one makes medical products; one operates fast-food restaurants; and two are relatively mundane manufacturers of mechanical and electrical products. But each is a hands-on operator, not a holding company or a conglomerate. And while not every plan succeeds, in the day-to-day pursuit of their business these companies succeed far more often than they fail. And they succeed because of their management's almost instinctive adherence to the eight attributes.

Bias Toward Action

In each of these companies, the key instructions are *do it, fix it, try it.* They avoid analyzing and questioning products to death, and they avoid complicated procedures for developing new ideas. Controlled experiments abound in these companies. The attitude of management is to "get some data, do it, then adjust it," rather than to wait for a perfect overall plan. The companies tend to be tinkerers rather than inventors, making small steps of progress rather than conceiving sweeping new concepts. At McDonald's Corp., for example, the objective is to do the little things regularly and well.

Ideas are solicited regularly and tested quickly. Those that work are pushed fast; those that don't are discarded just as quickly. At 3M Co., the management never kills an idea without trying it out; it just goes on the back burner.

These managements avoid long, complicated business plans or new projects. At 3M, for example, new product ideas must be proposed in less than five pages. At Procter & Gamble Co., one-page memos are the rule, but every figure in a P&G memo can be relied on unfailingly.

To ensure that they achieve results, these companies set a few well-defined goals for their managers. At Texas Instruments Inc., for one, a typical goal would be a set date for having a new plant operating or for having a designated percent of a sales force call on customers in a new market. A TI executive explained: "We've experimented a lot, but the bottom line for any senior manager is the maxim that more than two objectives is no objective."

These companies have learned to focus quickly on problems. One method is to appoint a "czar" who has responsibility for one problem across the company. At Digital Equipment Corp. and Hewlett-Packard Co., for example, there are software czars, because customer demand for programming has become the key issue for the future growth of those companies. Du Pont Co., when it discovered it was spending $800 million a year on transportation, set up a logistics czar. Other companies have productivity czars or energy czars with the power to override a manufacturing division's autonomy.

Another tool is the task force. But these companies tend to use the task force in an unusual way. Task forces are authorized to fix things, not to generate reports and paper. At Digital Equipment TI, H-P, and 3M, task forces have a short duration, seldom more than 90 days. Says a Digital Equipment executive: "When we've got a big problem here, we grab 10 senior guys and stick them in a room for a week. They come up with an answer and implement it." All members are volunteers, and they tend to be senior managers rather than junior people ordered to serve. Management espouses the busy-member theory: "We don't want people on task forces who want to become permanent task force members. We only put people on them who are so busy that their major objective is to get the problem solved and to get back to their main jobs." Every task force at TI is disbanded after its work is done, but within three months the senior operations committee formally reviews and assesses the results. TI demands that the managers who requested and ran the task force justify the time spent on it. If the task force turns out to have been useless, the manager is chided publicly, a painful penalty in TI's peer-conscious culture.

Simple Form and Lean Staff

Although all ten of these companies are big—the smallest McDonald's, has sales in excess of $1.9 billion—they are structured along "small is beautiful" lines. Emerson Electric, 3M, J&J, and H-P are divided into small entrepreneurial units that—although smaller than economies of scale might suggest—manage to get things done. No H-P division, for example, ever employs more than 1,200 people. TI, with 90 product customer centers, keeps each notably autonomous.

Within the units themselves, activities are kept to small, manageable groups. At Dana Corp., small teams work on productivity improvement. At the high-technology companies, small autonomous teams, headed by a product "champion," shepherd ideas through the corporate bureaucracy to ensure that they quickly receive attention from the top.

Staffs are also kept small to avoid bureaucracies. Fewer than 100 people help run Dana, a $3 billion corporation. Digital Equipment and Emerson are also noted for small staffs.

Closeness to the Customer

The well-managed companies are customer driven—not technology driven, not product driven, not strategy driven. Constant contact with the customer pro-

HOW 10 WELL-RUN COMPANIES PERFORMED IN 1979

	Sales	Profits	Return on	Return on
	Millions of Dollars		Sales	Equity
IBM	$22,862.8	$3,011.3	14.8%	21.6%
Procter & Gamble	10,080.6	615.7	5.6	19.3
3M	5,440.3	655.2	12.2	24.4
Johnson & Johnson	4,211.6	352.1	6.5	19.6
Texas Instruments	3,224.1	172.9	5.1	19.2
Dana	2,789.0	165.8	6.1	19.3
Emerson Electric	2,749.9	208.8	7.5	21.5
Hewlett-Packard	2,361.0	203.0	8.2	18.1
Digital Equipment	2,031.6	207.5	9.7	19.7
McDonald's	1,937.9	188.6	8.7	22.5
BW Composite of 1,200 Companies			5.1	16.6

vides insights that direct the company. Says one executive, "Where do you start? Not by poring over abstract market research. You start by getting out there with the customer." In a study of two fast-paced industries (scientific instruments and component manufacturing), Eric Von Hippel, associate professor at Massachusetts Institute of Technology, found that 100% of the major new product ideas—and 80% of the minor new product variations—came directly from customers.

At both IBM and Digital Equipment, top management spends at least 30 days a year conferring with top customers. No manager at IBM holds a staff job for more than three years, except in the legal, finance, and personnel departments. The reason: IBM believes that staff people are out of the mainstream because they do not meet with customers regularly.

Both companies use customer-satisfaction surveys to help determine management's compensation. Another company spends 12% of its research and development budget on sending engineers and scientists out to visit customers. One R&D chief spends two months each year with customers. At Lanier Business Products Inc., another fast growing company, the 20 most senior executives make sales calls every month.

Staying close to the customer means sales and service overkill. "Assistants to" at IBM are assigned to senior executives with the sole function of processing customer complaints within 24 hours. At Digital Equipment, J&J, IBM, and 3M, immense effort is expended to field an extraordinary well-trained sales force. Caterpillar Tractor Co., another company considered to have excellent management, spends much of its managerial talent on efforts to make a reality of its motto, "24-hour parts delivery anywhere in the world."

These companies view the customer as an integral element of their businesses. A bank officer who started his career as a J&J accountant recalls that he was required to make customer calls even though he was in a financial department. The reason: to ensure that he understood the customer's perspective and could handle a proposal with empathy.

Productivity Improvement via Consensus

One way to get productivity increases is to install new capital equipment. But another method is often overlooked. Productivity can be improved by motivating and stimulating employees. One way to do that is to give them autonomy. At TI, shop floor teams set their own targets for production. In the years since the company has used this approach, executives say, workers have set goals that require them to stretch but that are reasonable and attainable.

The key is to motivate all of the people involved in each process. At 3M, for example, a team that includes technologists, marketers, production people, and financial types is formed early in a new product venture. It is self-sufficient and stays together from the inception to the national introduction. Although 3M is aware that this approach can lead to redundancy, it feels that the team spirit and motivation make it worthwhile.

Almost all of these companies use "corny" but effective methods to reward their workers. Badges, pins, and medals are all part of such recognition programs. Outstanding production teams at TI are invited to describe their successes to the board, as a form of recognition. Significantly, the emphasis is never only on monetary awards.

Autonomy To Encourage Entrepreneurship

A company cannot encourage entrepreneurship if it holds its managers on so tight a leash that they cannot make decisions. Well-managed companies authorize their managers to act like entrepreneurs. Dana, for one, calls this method the "store manager" concept. Plant managers are free to make purchasing decisions and to start productivity programs on their own. As a result, these managers develop unusual programs with results that far exceed those of a division or corporate staff. And the company has a grievance rate that is a fraction of the average reported by the United Auto Workers for all the plants it represents.

The successful companies rarely will force their managers to go against their own judgment. At 3M, TI, IBM, and J&J, decisions on product promotion are not based solely on market potential. An important factor in the decision is the zeal and drive of the volunteer who champions a product. Explains one executive at TI: "In every instance of a new product failure, we had forced someone into championing it involuntarily."

The divisional management is generally responsible for replenishing its new product array. In these well-managed companies, headquarters staff may not cut off funds for divisional products arbitrarily. What is more, the divisions are allowed to reinvest most of their earnings in their own operations. Although this flies in the face of the product-portfolio concept, which dictates that a corporate chief milk mature divisions to feed those with apparently greater growth potential, these companies recognize that entrepreneurs will not be developed in corporations that give the fruits of managers' labor to someone else.

Almost all these companies strive to place new products into separate start-up divisions. A manager is more likely to be recognized—and promoted—for pushing a hot new product out of his division to enable it to stand on its own than he is for simply letting his own division get overgrown.

Possibly most important at these companies, entrepreneurs are both encouraged and honored at all staff levels. TI, for one, has created a special group of "listeners"—138 senior technical people called "individual contributors"—to assess new ideas. Junior staff members are particularly encouraged to bring their ideas to one of these individuals for a one-on-one evaluation. Each "contributor" has the authority to approve substantial start-up funds ($20,000 to $30,000) for product experimentation. TI's successful Speak'n'Spell device was developed this way.

IBM's Fellows Program serves a similar purpose, although it is intended to permit proven senior performers to explore their ideas rather than to open communication lines for bright comers. Such scientists have at their beck and call thousands of IBM's technical people. The Fellows tend to be highly skilled gadflies, people who can shake things up—almost invariably for the good of the company.

The operating principle at well-managed companies is to do one thing well. At IBM, the all-pervasive value is customer service. At Dana it is productivity improvement. At 3M and H-P, it is new product development. At P&G it is product quality. At McDonald's it is customer service—quality, cleanliness, and value.

Stress on a Key Business Value

At all these companies, the values are pursued with an almost religious zeal by the chief executive officers. Rene McPherson, now dean of Stanford University's Graduate School of Business but until recently Dana's CEO, incessantly preached cost reduction and productivity improvement—and the company doubled its productivity in seven years. Almost to the day when Thomas Watson Jr. retired from IBM he wrote memos to the staff on the subject of calling on customers—even stressing the proper dress for the call. TI's ex-chairman Patrick Haggerty made it a point to drop in at a development laboratory on his way home each night when he was in Dallas. And in another company, where competitive position was the prime focus, one division manager wrote 700 memos to his subordinates one year, analyzing competitors.

Such single-minded focus on a value becomes a culture for the company. Nearly every IBM employee has stories about how he or she took great pains to solve a customer's problem. New product themes even dominate 3M and H-P lunchroom conversations. Every operational review at H-P focuses on new products, with a minimum amount of time devoted to financial results or projections—because President John Young has made it clear that he believes that proper implementation of new-product plans automatically creates the right numbers. In fact, Young makes it a point to start new employees in the new-product process and keep them there for a few years as part of a "socialization" pattern. "I don't care if they do come from the Stanford Business Schoool," he says. "For a few years they get their hands dirty, or we are not interested." At McDonald's the company's values are drummed into employees at Hamburger U., a training program every employee goes through.

As the employees who are steeped in the corporate culture move up the ladder, they become role models for newcomers, and the process continues. It is possibly best exemplified by contrast. American Telephone & Telegraph Co., which recently began to develop a marketing orientation, has been hamstrung in its efforts because of a lack of career telephone executives with marketing successes. When Archie J. McGill was hired from IBM to head AT&T's marketing, some long-term employees balked at his leadership because he "wasn't one of them," and so was not regarded as a model.

Another common pitfall for companies is the sending of mixed signals to line managers. One company has had real problems introducing new products despite top management's constant public stress on innovation—simply because line managers perceived the real emphasis to be on cost-cutting. They viewed top management as accountants who refused to invest or to take risks, and they consistently proposed imitative products. At another company, where the CEO insisted that his major thrust was new products, an analysis of how he spent his time over a three-month period showed that no more than 5% of his efforts were directed to new products. His stated emphasis therefore was not credible. Not surprisingly, his employees never picked up the espoused standard.

Too many messages, even when sincerely meant, can cause the same problem. One CEO complained that no matter how hard he tried to raise what he regarded as an unsatisfactory quality level he was unsuccessful. But when McKinsey questioned his subordinates, they said, "Of course he's for quality, but he's for everything else, too. We have a theme a month here." The outstanding companies, in contrast, have one theme and stick to it.

Sticking to What They Know Best

Robert W. Johnson, the former chairman of J&J, put it this way: "Never acquire any business you don't know how to run." Edward G. Harness, CEO at P&G, says, "This company has never left its base." All of the successful companies have been able to define their strengths—marketing, customer contact, new-product innovation, low-cost manufacturing—and then build on them. They have resisted the temptation to move into new businesses that look attractive but require corporate skills they do not have.

Simultaneous Loose-Tight Controls

While this may sound like a contradiction, it is not. The successful companies control a few variables tightly, but allow flexibility and looseness in others. 3M uses return on sales and number of employees as yard sticks for control. Yet it gives management lots of leeway in day-to-day operations. When McPherson became president of Dana, he threw out all of the company's policy manuals and substituted a one-page philosophy statement and a control system that required divisions to report costs and revenues on a daily basis.

IBM probably has the classic story about flexible controls. After the company suffered well-publicized and costly problems with its System 360 computer several years ago—problems that cost hundreds of millions of dollars to fix—Watson ordered Frank T. Cary, then a vice-president, to incorporate a system of checks and balances in new-product testing. The system made IBM people so cautious that they stopped taking risks. When Cary became president of IBM, one of the first things he did to reverse that attitude was to loosen some of the controls. He recognized that the new system would indeed prevent such an expensive problem from ever happening again, but its rigidity would also keep IBM from ever developing another major system.

By sticking to these eight basics, the successful companies have achieved better-than-average growth. Their managements are able not only to change but also to change quickly. They keep their sights aimed externally at their customers and competitors, and not on their own financial reports.

Excellence in management takes brute perseverance—time, repetition, and simplicity. The tools include plant visits, internal memos, and focused systems. Ignoring these rules may mean that the company slowly loses its vitality, its growth flattens, and its competitiveness is lost.

Reading V
Corporate
Culture

The
hard-to-change values
that spell
success or failure

Five years ago the chief executives of two major oil companies determined that they would have to diversify out of oil because their current business could not support long-term growth and it faced serious political threats. Not only did they announce their new long-range strategies to employees and the public, but they established elaborate plans to implement them. Today, after several years of floundering in attempts to acquire and build new businesses, both companies are firmly back in oil, and the two CEOs have been replaced.

Each of the CEOs had been unable to implement his strategy, not because it was theoretically wrong or bad but because neither had understood that his company's culture was so entrenched in the traditions and values of doing business as oilmen that employees resisted—and sabotaged—the radical changes that the CEOs tried to impose. Oil operations require long-term investments for long term rewards; but the new businesses needed short-term views and an emphasis on current returns. Successes had come from hitting it big in wild-catting; but the new success was to be based on such abstractions as market share or numbers growth—all seemingly nebulous concepts to them. Too late did the CEOs realize that strategies can only be implemented with the whole-hearted effort and belief of everyone involved. If implementing them violates employees' basic beliefs about their roles in the company, or the traditions that underlie the corporation's culture, they are doomed to fail.

Culture implies values, such as aggressiveness, defensiveness, or nimble-ness, that set a pattern for a company's activities, opinions, and actions. That pattern is instilled in employees by managers' example and passed down to succeeding generations of workers. The CEO's words alone do not produce culture; rather, his actions and those of his managers do.

A corporation's culture can be its major strength when it is consistent with its strategies. Some of the most successful companies have clearly demonstrated that fact, including:

- International Business Machines Corp., where marketing drives a service philosophy that is almost unparalleled. The company keeps a hot line open 24 hours a day, seven days a week, to service IBM products.
- International Telephone & Telegraph Corp., where financial discipline demands total dedication. To beat out the competitition in a merger, an executive once called former Chairman Harold S. Geneen at 3 a.m. to get his approval.
- Digital Equipment Corp., where an emphasis on innovation creates freedom with responsibility. Employees can set their own hours and working style, but they are expected to articulate and support their activities with evidence of progress.
- Delta Air Lines Inc., where a focus on customer service produces a high degree of teamwork. Employees will substitute in other jobs to keep planes flying and baggage moving.
- Atlantic Richfield Co., where an emphasis on entrepreneurship encourages action. Operating men have the autonomy to bid on promising fields without hierarchical approval.

But a culture that prevents a company from meeting competitive threats, or from adapting to changing economic or social environments, can lead to the company's stagnation and ultimate demise unless it makes a conscious effort to change. One that did make this effort is PepsiCo Inc., where the cultural emphasis has been systematically changed over the past two decades from passivity to aggressiveness.

Once the company was content in its No. 2 spot, offering Pepsi as a cheaper alternative to Coca-Cola. But today, a new employee at PepsiCo quickly learns that beating the competition, whether outside or inside the company, is the surest path to success. In its soft-drink operation, for example, Pepsi's marketers now take on Coke directly, asking consumers to compare the taste of the two colas. That direct confrontation is reflected inside the company as well. Managers are pitted against each other to grab more market share, to work harder, and to wring more profits out of their businesses. Because winning is the key value at Pepsi, losing has its penalties. Consistent runners-up find their jobs gone. Employees know they must win merely to stay in place—and must devastate the competition to get ahead.

But the aggressive competitor who succeeds at Pepsi would be sorely out of place at J. C. Penney Co., where a quick victory is far less important than building long-term loyalty. Indeed, a Penney store manager once was severely rebuked by the company's president for making too much profit. That was considered unfair to customers, whose trust Penney seeks to win. The business style set by the company's founder—which one competitor describes as avoiding "taking unfair advantage of anyone the company did business with"—still prevails today. Customers know they can return merchandise with no questions asked; suppliers know that Penney will not haggle over terms; and employees are comfortable in their jobs, knowing that Penney will avoid layoffs at all costs and will find easier jobs for those who cannot handle more demanding ones. Not surprisingly, Penney's average executive tenure is 33 years while Pepsi's is 10.

These vastly different methods of doing business are but two examples of corporate culture. People who work at Pepsi and Penney sense that the corporate values are the yardstick by which they will be measured. Just as tribal cultures have totems and taboos that dictate how each member will act toward fellow members and outsiders, so does a corporation's culture influence employees' actions toward customers, competitors, suppliers, and one another. Sometimes the rules are written out. More often they are tacit. Most often, they are laid down by a strong founder and hardened by success into custom.

"Culture gives people a sense of how to behave and what they ought to be doing," explains Howard M. Schwartz, vice-president of Management Analysis Center Inc., a Cambridge (Mass.) consulting firm that just completed a study of corporate culture. Indeed, so firmly are certain values entrenched in a company's behavior that predictable responses can be counted on not only by its employees but by its competitors. "How will our competitors behave?" is a stock question that strategic planners ask when contemplating a new move. The answers come from assessing competitors' time-honored priorities, their reactions to competition, and their ability to change course.

Because a company's culture is so pervasive, changing it becomes one of the most difficult tasks that any chief executive can undertake. Just as a primitive tribe's survival depended on its ability to react to danger, and to alter its way of life when necessary, so must corporations, faced with changing economic, social, and political climates, sometimes radically change their methods of operating. What stands in the way is not only the "relative immutability of culture," as the MAC study points out, but also the fact that few executives consciously recognize what their company's culture is and how it manifests itself. The concept of culture, says Stanley M. Davis, professor of organization behavior at Boston University and a co-author of the MAC study, is hard to understand. "It's like putting your hand in a cloud," he says.

Thomas J. Peters, a principal in McKinsey & Co., cites a client who believed it was imperative to his company's survival to add a marketing effort to his manufacturing-oriented organization. Because the company had no experts in marketing, it wanted to hire some. Consultants pointed out that this strategy would fail because all of the issues raised at company meetings concerned cost-cutting and production—never competition or customers. Rewards were built into achieving efficiencies in the first category, while none were built into understanding the second. Ultimately, the CEO recognized that he had to educate himself and his staff so thoroughly in marketing that he could build his own in-house team.

Similarly, American Telephone & Telegraph Co. is now trying to alter its service-oriented operation to give equal weight to marketing. Past attempts to do so ignored the culture and failed. For example, in 1961, AT&T set up a school to teach managers to coordinate the design and manufacture of data products for customized sales. But when managers completed the course, they found that the traditional way of operating—making noncustomized mass sales—were what counted in the company. They were given neither the time to analyze individual customers' needs nor rewards commensurate with such efforts. The result was that 85% of the graduates quit, and AT&T disbanded the school.

AT&T prides itself on its service operation, and with good reason. It provides the most efficient and broadest telephone system in the world, and it reacts to disaster with a speed unknown anywhere else. In 1975, for example, a fire swept through a switching center in lower Manhattan, knocking out service to 170,000 telephones. AT&T rallied 4,000 employees and shipped in 3,000 tons of equipment to restore full service in just 22 days—a task that could have taken a lesser company more than a year.

But costs for AT&T's service had been readily passed to customers through rate increases granted by public service commissions. Keeping costs down was thus never a major consideration. Now, however, since the Federal Communications Commission has decided to allow other companies to sell products in AT&T's once-captive markets, AT&T must change the orientation of its 1 million employees. In numbers alone, such a change is unprecedented in corporate history. Still, to survive in its new environment, Bell must alter its plans, strategies, and employee expectations of what the company wants from them, as well as their belief in the security of their jobs and old way of doing business.

To make the changes, Bell has analyzed its new requirements in exquisite detail that fills thousands of pages. It acknowledges its lack of skills in certain crucial areas: marketing, cost control, and administrative ability to deal with change. The company had rewarded managers who administered set policies by the book; today it is promoting innovators with advanced degrees in business administration. Once it measured service representatives by the speed with which they responded to calls; today they are measured by the number of problems they solve.

AT&T's new role model

Instead of its traditional policy of promoting from within, some new role models were hired from outside the company. Archie J. McGill, a former executive of International Business Machines Corp., was made vice-president of business marketing, for example. McGill is described by associates as an innovator who is the antithesis of the traditional "Bell-shaped man" because of his "combative, adversarial style." Just as IBM's slogan, "Think," encouraged its employees to be problem-solvers, McGill is hammering a new slogan, "I make the difference," into each of his marketers encouraging them to become entrepreneurs. That idea is reinforced by incentives that pit salespeople against each other for bonuses, a system unknown at Bell before.

Even so, the changes are slow. Learning to become solution-sellers has produced "a tremendous amount of confusion" among Bell marketing people, reports one large corporate customer. For example, AT&T is "absolutely trapped" if a customer requests an extra editing part for its standard teletype system, he says. "If you want something they don't have, they tend to solve the problem by saying, 'Let's go out for a drink'."

Even McGill concedes that "anytime you have an orientation toward consulting [past practices] as opposed to being adaptive to a situation, change doesn't happen overnight." Bell's director of planning, W. Brooke Tunstall, estimates that it will take another three to five years to attain an 85% change in the company's orientation. Still, he insists, there has already been "a definite change in mindset at the upper levels." The arguments heard around the company now concern the pace of change rather than its scope. Says Tunstall, "I haven't run into anyone who doesn't understand why the changes are needed."

The AT&T example clearly demonstrates the need for a company to examine its existing culture in depth and to acknowledge the reasons for revolutionary change, if changes must be made. As AT&T learned from its earlier attempt to sell specialized services, change cannot be implemented merely by sending people to school. Nor can it be made by hiring new staff, by acquiring new businesses, by changing the name of the company, or by redefining its business. Even exhortations by the chief executive to operate differently will not succeed unless they are backed up by a changed structure, new role models, new incentive systems, and new rewards and punishments built into operations.

A chief executive, for example, who demands innovative new products from his staff, but who leaves in place a hierarchy that can smother a good new idea at its first airing, is unlikely to get what he wants. In contrast, an unwritten, rule at 3M Co., says one manager, is, "Never be responsible for killing an idea." Similarly, if a CEO's staff knows that his first priority is consistent earnings growth, it will be unlikely to present him with any new product or service idea, no matter how great its potential, if it requires a long incubation period and a drag on earnings before it reaches fruition. At Pillsbury Co., for example, managers are afraid to suggest ideas for products that might require considerable research and development because they know that Chairman William H. Spoor is obsessed with improving short-term financial results, sources say.

The real priorities

One element is certain: Employees cannot be fooled. They understand the real priorities in the corporation. At the first inconsistency they will become confused, then reluctant to change, and finally intransigent. Indeed, consistency in every aspect of a culture is essential to its success, as PepsiCo's transformation into an archrival of Coke shows.

For decades, Coke's unchallenged position in the market was so complete that the brand name Coke became synonymous with cola drinks. It attained this distinction under Robert W. Woodruff, who served as chief executive for 32 years and is still chairman of the company's finance committee at age 90. Woodruff had an "almost messianic drive to get Coca-Cola [drunk] all over the world," says Harvey Z. Yazijian, coauthor of the forthcoming book, *The Cola Wars.* So successful was Coke in accomplishing this under Woodruff—and later, J. Paul Austin, who will retire in March as CEO—that Coca-Cola became known as "America's second State Dept." Its trademark became a symbol of American life itself.

"A real problem in the past," says Yazijian, "was that they had a lot of deadwood" among employees. Nevertheless, Coke's marketing and advertising were extremely effective in expanding consumption of the product. But the lack of serious competition and the company's relative isolation in its home town of Atlanta allowed it to become "fat, dumb, and happy," according to one consultant. Coke executives are known to be extremely loyal to the company and circumspect to the point of secrecy in their dealings with the outside world.

In the mid-1950s, Pepsi, once a sleepy New York-based bottler with a lame slogan, "Twice as much for a nickel, too," began to develop into a serious threat under the leadership of Chairman Alfred N. Steele. The movement gathered momentum, and by the early 1970s the company had become a ferocious competitor under Chairman Donald M. Kendall and President Andrall E. Pearson, a former director of McKinsey. The culture that these two executives determined to create was based on the goal of becoming the No. 1 marketer of soft drinks.

Severe pressure was put on managers to show continual improvement in market share, product volume, and profits. "Careers ride on tenths of a market share point," says John Sculley, vice-president and head of domestic beverage operations. This atmosphere pervades the company's nonbeverage units as well. "Everyone knows that if the results aren't there, you had better have your resume up to date," says a former snack food manager.

To keep everyone on their toes, a "creative tension" is continually nurtured among departments at Pepsi, says another former executive. The staff is kept lean and managers are moved to new jobs constantly, which results in people working long hours and engaging in political maneuvering "just to keep their jobs from being reorganized out from under them," says a headhunter.

Kendall himself sets a constant example. He once resorted to using a snowmobile to get to work in a blizzard, demonstrating the ingenuity and dedication to work he expects from his staff. This type of pressure has pushed many managers out. But a recent company survey shows that others thrive under such conditions. "Most of our guys are having fun," Pearson insists. They are the kind of people, elaborates Sculley, who "would rather be in the Marines than in the Army."

Like Marines, Pepsi executives are expected to be physically fit as well as mentally alert: Pepsi employs four physical-fitness instructors at its headquarters, and a former executive says it is an unwritten rule that to get ahead in the company a manager must stay in shape. The company encourages one-on-one sports as well as interdepartmental competition in such games as soccer and basketball. In company team contests or business dealings, says Sculley, "the more competitive it becomes, the more we enjoy it." In such a culture, less competitive managers are deliberately weeded out. Even suppliers notice a difference today. "They are smart, sharp negotiators who take advantage of all opportunities," says one.

While Pepsi steadily gained market share in the 1970s, Coke was reluctant to admit that a threat existed, Yazijian says. Pepsi now has bested Coke in the domestic take-home market, and it is mounting a challenge overseas. At the moment, the odds are in favor of Coke, which sells one-third of the world's soft drinks and has had Western Europe locked up for years. But Pepsi has been making inroads: Besides monopolizing the Soviet market, it has dominated the Arab Middle East ever since Coke was ousted in 1967, when it granted a bottling franchise in Israel. Still, Coke showed that it was not giving up. It cornered a potentially vast new market—China.

With Pepsi gaining domestic market share faster than Coke—last year it gained 7.5% vs. Coke's 5%—observers believe that Coke will turn more to foreign sales or food sales for growth. Roberto C. Goizueta, who will be Coke's next chairman, will not reveal Coke's strategy. But one tactic the company has already used is hiring away some of the Pepsi's "tigers." Coke has lured Donald Breen, Jr., who played a major role in developing the "Pepsi Challenge"—the consumer taste test—as well as five other marketing and sales executives associated with Pepsi. Pepsi won its court battle to prevent Breen from revealing confidential information over the next 12 months. But the company's current culture is unlikely to build loyalty. Pepsi may well have to examine the dangers of cultivating ruthlessness in its managers, say former executives.

Quite a different problem faces J. C. Penney today. Its well-entrenched culture, laid down by founder James Cash Penney in a seven-point codification of the company's guiding principles, called "The Penney Idea," has brought it tremendous loyalty from its staff but lower profits recently. Its introduction of fashionable apparel has been only partially successful, because customers identify it with nonfashionable staples, such as children's clothes, work clothes, and hardware. It has also been outpaced in the low end of the market by aggressive discounters, such as K Mart Corp., which knocked Penney out of the No. 2 retailer's spot in 1976 and which has been gaining market share at Penney's expense ever since.

Penney's is proud that two national magazines cited it as one of the 10 best places to work in the nation, a claim that is borne out by employees. "Everyone is treated as an individual," notes one former executive. Another praises the company's "bona fide participative" decision-making process, and adds that Penney has "an openness in the organization that many large companies don't seem to achieve."

But Penney's paternalistic attitude toward its work force has meant that it always tries to find new jobs for marginally competent employees rather than firing them, says Stephen Temlock, manager of human resource strategy development. He concedes that some workers "expect us to be papa and mama, and aren't motivated enough to help themselves." The corollary of that, he admits, is that the company sometimes fails to reward outstanding performers enough.

Penney's entrenched culture makes any change slow, Temlock adds, but he insists that this solidity helps to maintain a balance between "an out-and-out aggressive environment and a human environment." Penney Chairman Donald V. Seibert believes that the company's problems have more to do with the retailing industry's endemic cyclicality than with company culture. Although he admits that he worries sometimes that the company is too inbred, he notes that it has brought in different types of people in the last several years as it entered new businesses, such as catalog sales and insurance. Seibert adds that the company firmly believes that the principles of "The Penney Idea" will be relevant no matter how much the economic environment changes. "You can't say that there's a good way to modernize integrity," he emphasizes.

Seibert may be right. One competitor notes that the aggressive newcomers in retailing have profited from older retailers' mistakes, and thus have found shortcuts to growth. But, says this source, "the shortcuts are limited, and the newcomers' staying power has yet to be proven." Still, if the new threat continues, Penney's pace must speed up, and it must soon act more flexibly to protect itself; it may even have to abandon some of the customs that have grown up around its humanistic principles.

Another gentlemanly company found that it had to do just that to regain its leading position in banking. Chase Manhattan Bank had cruised along comfortably for years, leaning on the aristocratic image of its chairman, David Rockefeller. In the mid-1970s, however, Chase was jolted out of its lethargy by a sharp skid in earnings and a return on assets that plunged as low as 0.24% in 1976. Its real estate portfolio was loaded with questionable and sour loans, and its commercial lending department's reputation had been severely tarnished because high turnover of its lending officers and the resulting inexperience of those who replaced them made the bank less responsive to customers. Some embarrassing questions about Chase's basic management practices began to be raised.

Rockefeller and a group of top executives, including Willard C. Butcher, now chief executive and chairman-elect, decided that the fault lay with a culture that rewarded people more for appearance than performance and that produced inbreeding and a smugness that made the bank loath to grapple with competitors. The typical Chase executive in those days was a well-groomed functionary who did not drive himself hard or set high standards for his own performance, banking analysts remember.

The first step toward change, Chase executives felt, was for the bank to define what it wanted to be. Early in 1977 it drew up a three-page mission statement that outlined the company's business mix. "We will only do those things we can do extremely well and with the highest level of integrity," the statement said. For Chase, this meant taking a hard look at some unprofitable parts of its business. Subsequently, it closed some 50 low-volume domestic branches in New York, and it began to turn away questionable loan business that it had accepted before.

The mission statement also spelled out specific targets for financial goals, such as return on equity and assets and debt-to-capital ratio. At the start, employees doubted that the company could meet these goals; one, for example, was a return on assets of 0.55% to 0.65%, more than double the 1976 figure.

Chase began a major effort to step up communications between top management and the rest of the staff. This was a departure from the old days, when decisions were simply handed down from the 17th-floor executive suite, says one former manager. The participation of all employees created a sense of "ownership" of the program by all, something consultant Robert F. Allen, president of the Human Resources Institute in Morristown, N.J., believes is essential to any long-lasting change.

Like AT&T, Chase promoted new role models, such as Richard J. Boyle, now a senior vice-president, who took over the bank's troubled real estate operations at age 32. Boyle, described as a "workaholic" with strong opinions and a willingness to make hard decisions, such as writing off floundering projects rather than carrying them on the company's books, is the antithesis of the old-style Chase banker, analysts say. To run commercial lending, the bank lured back James H. Carey, who had left Chase for Hambros Bank. "They put absolutely brilliant people in problem areas," remarks John J. Mason, banking analyst at Shearson Loeb Rhoades Inc.

Rewards for performers

But tradition suffered: One-third of the bank's top-executives were replaced by outsiders. Salaries and incentive payments were overhauled to provide greater rewards for top performers. And an advanced management course was started for promising young managers. The culture has been altered from its emphasis on style to a focus on performance. And now that employees' expectations of the company have changed, the new order is likely to prevail. But even Butcher, although pleased with the improvement, warns, "The danger is always that you become complacent."

Chase was able to effect the change in its culture under the aegis of its reigning leaders, Rockefeller and Butcher. But some companies find that the

EVIDENCE OF CULTURAL CHANGE IN A BETTER BOTTOM LINE

	1976	1979
	Millions of Dollars	
Assets	$45,638	$64,708
Deposits	33,808	44,725
Loans	30,663	40,170
Interest income	2,711	5,639
Net chargeoffs for bad loans	269	93
Net income	116	303

Data: Chase Manhattan Corp. annual reports

only way to solve problems is to bring in a new chief who can implement sweeping change. Yet even a new strongman can run up against a wall unless he understands the company's existing culture.

Dennis C. Stanfill, a corporate finance specialist, ran into just such problems when he took over as chief executive in 1971 at Twentieth Century-Fox Film Corp. Stanfill's aim was to balance the risks of the motion picture business with steady earnings from other leisure-time businesses, which he began acquiring. But he also insisted on running all of Fox's businesses, including the film operation, on an equal basis by keeping the corporate purse strings pulled tight—and in his hands.

What Stanfill overlooked was that creative people require a different kind of managing than do typical business employees. While the latter group can usually be motivated by using the carrot-and-stick approach, creative people are self-motivated. They will work as hard as needed to perform as perfectly as they can, because they identify their work not with the company but with themselves. What they want from their patron-managers, however, is applause and rewards for a good job, and protection when they bomb.

Stanfill violated those expectations when he refused to give Alan Ladd Jr., president of the film group, control over bonuses for his staff, which had produced such hits as *Star Wars*. From Stanfill's point of view, the decision was sound: In just three years he had erased a $125 million bank debt and brought the company into the black after it had been in default on its loans. He believed the traditional extravagances of the film company would keep the corporation on a shaky foundation. Indeed, he says he wants "to keep the balance between show and business."

Not a 'brokerage'

But the film company's response was predictable. Ladd quit to start his own operation, taking several key people with him. "In my opinion, Stanfill doesn't understand what motivates creative people," says Ladd. "You don't run a film business like a brokerage house."

Fox's directors quickly stepped in and demanded that Stanfill find a "name" replacement for Ladd. Stanfill has since picked Alan J. Hirschfield, who had been laid off by Columbia Pictures Industries Inc. and who has been praised by the industry for adding a creative spark to Fox this past year. But Stanfill now must make financial decisions jointly with Hirschfield.

Whether Stanfill will ever be comfortable in such a high-risk business remains questionable. One film industry analyst thinks not. He says: "Stanfill has never felt comfortable running an entertainment company. He is downside-risk-oriented on motion pictures, and didn't know why Ladd was so successful." If that is true, Stanfill could be on a collision course with Fox's implicit culture.

Stanfill may have recognized that the strategy he was imposing on Fox's film business, which produces 63% of the corporation's pretax operating earnings, violated its culture. But he obviously believed that it was necessary for the company's survival. He has not, however, changed Fox's culture. As more and more chief executives recognize the need for long-range strategies, they will have to consider the effects of these strategies on their companies. It may well be that CEOs must then decide whether their strategies must change to fit their companies' culture or the cultures must change to assure survival.

Reading VI
Type Z Organization*:

A corporate alternative to village life

William G. Ouchi and Alfred M. Jaeger

Now all the evidence of psychiatry . . . shows
that membership in a group sustains a man,
enables him to maintain his equilibrium under
the ordinary shocks of life, and helps him to
bring up children who will in turn be happy and
resilient. If his group is shattered around him, if
he leaves a group in which he was a valued
member, and if, above all, he finds no new
group to which he can relate himself, he will
under stress, develop disorders of thought,
feeling, and behavior . . . . The cycle is vicious;
loss of group membership in one generation
may make men less capable of group
membership in the next. The civilization that, by
its very process of growth, shatters small group
life will leave men and women lonely and
unhappy.

George C. Homans, The Human Group

*This paper is based on "Type Z Organization: Stability in the Midst of Mobility" which
will be published in the *Academy of Management Review* in 1978. This research is supported
by a grant from the Alcoa Foundation.

Society has traditionally relied upon kinship, neighborhood, church, and family networks to provide the social support and anchors which organized our society and made collective life possible. As Elton Mayo pointed out in *The Social Problems of an Industrial Civilization* (1945), the advent of the factory system of production and the rapid rate of technological change have produced high rates of urbanization, mobility, and division of labor. The effect of these forces has been to weaken the community, family, church, and friendship ties of many Americans. Many social observers point to the weakening of associational ties as the basic cause of increasing rates of alcoholism, divorce, crime, and other symptoms of mental illness at a societal level.

The argument that increasing size, density, and heterogeneity of cities leads to many forms of social disorganization is not new. The large organization which brought about urbanization and its consequent social ills, however, can also provide relief from them.

With memories of the totalitarian paternalism of the mines and the plantations still not healed by time, Americans have been reluctant to even consider the work organization as the social umbrella under which people can live lives that are free, happy, and productive. The ideology of independence that is part of the basic fabric of America recoils at the thought of individual freedom subordinated to collective commitment. American heroes are the rough, tough individualists, the John Waynes, the Evel Knievels, the Gloria Steinems. Our most pitiable figures are those who lose their individuality in some larger, corporate entity and become organization men, faceless men in gray flannel suits.

But there is a paradox in the American spirit; for millions of Americans still admire the stable, collective, nonindividual style of life expressed in such television favorites as "The Waltons," "Little House on the Prairie," "Bonanza," and others. The strength of cohesive groups is much desired and much admired. Americans enjoy the beauty of a well-coordinated football or basketball team, just as they can identify with the individual strength of a Jack Nicklaus or a Muhammad Ali.

The point is that while we worry over the disappearance of the family, the church, the neighborhood, and the friendship network, we have been blinded by our predispositions to the most likely alternative source of associational ties, of cohesion: the work organization. Employment already defines many aspects of our lives: our socio-economic status, our children's education, the kinds and lengths of vacations we take, the frequency and severity with which we can afford to become ill, and even the way in which pension benefits allow us to live our retirement years.

From childhood to the grave, the work organization plays a central role in identifying us and in molding our lives. We see in Japan, Poland, China, and other countries, models of work organization which provide such an organization of life and of society; but we have been unwilling to borrow these models, because they do not permit the individual freedom that is basic to American life. What we must discover is that uniquely American solution which allows individual freedom while using the work organization to support and encourage the stability of associational ties.

One author's previous research has indicated that the Japanese form of work organization was finding great acceptance in the U.S., while the American form is not at all successful in Japan.* Production workers up to top executives were interviewed at 25 companies, each of which has operations both in the U.S. and in Japan. Half of the companies were American corporations, and half were Japanese.

The increasingly familiar characteristics of Japanese companies were observed. These include almost total inclusion of the employee into the work organization so that the superior concerns himself with the personal and family life of each subordinate, a collective, nonindividual approach to work and to responsibility, and extremely high identification of the individual with his company. These characteristics are largely the result of the lifetime employment system which characterizes large companies in Japan; while 28.5% of males aged 20–24 in the U.S. change employers per year, the figure for Japan is 7.5%, most of which occurs in small companies.

The surprising finding was that Japanese companies opening operations in the U.S. are applying a slightly modified form of the pure Japanese type with some success. The typical Japanese company in the U.S. will have 3–5 top management officers from Japan, a like number of American executives, and perhaps 200 American blue-collar and technical employees. While those companies do not provide company housing or large bonuses as in Japan, they do attempt to create the same sort of complete inclusion of the employee into the company.

Operationally, that means that supervisors are taught to be aware of all aspects of an employee's life, that extra-work social life is often connected to other employees, that corporate values are adjusted to reflect employee needs as well as profit needs, and that high job security is protected above all else. The American employees expressed a great deal of liking for this "atmosphere" or "climate," with the managerial staff in particular noting the difference from their previous employers.

Individual Freedom and Group Cohesion

This study gave evidence that, while Americans probably do not ever want to return to old-style paternalism, they do favor a work organization which provides associational ties, stability, and job security. The Japanese-American mixed form suggested the model which may simultaneously permit individual freedom and group cohesion.

One important characteristic of the mixed model, different from either the Japanese or the American ideal types, was that the employee and his or her nuclear family are part of the organization. In Japan, while the work organization provides a total environment for the male employees, his family is totally excluded from interaction. His superior will aid him in finding a wife, will

---

*"Made in America (Under Japanese Management)," by Richard Tanner Johnson and William G. Ouchi, *Harvard Business Review,* Sept.–Oct. 1974.

know the names of his children, and will help him in family crises, but he will rarely if ever interact directly with them. This model works well in Japan because women and children have a society of their own based on family and school ties which are relatively permanent due to low rates of geographical and social mobility.

In the U.S., however, the company that provides a complete social existence for the employee but excludes his or her family will precipitate a crisis in which the employee will be torn between two competing loyalties. The spouse and children of the typical American employee have no relatives or lifelong friends living nearby, and no other associational ties to provide them with social support. Thus the mixed model succeeds by simultaneously providing such ties for both the employee and his or her family.

In the course of this research, it became apparent that there are some American companies which, by reputation, have many of the characteristics of this mixed model. Included in this group are Kodak, Cummins Engine Company, IBM, Levi Strauss, National Cash Register, Procter and Gamble, Utah International, and Minnesota Mining and Manufacturing (3M). In each case, the historical rates of turnover are low, loyalty and morale are reputed to be very high, and identification with the company is reputed to be strong.

In addition, it is notable that each of these companies has been among the most successful of American companies for many decades, a record which strongly suggests that something about the form of organization, rather than a particular product or market position, has kept the organization vital and strong. It is also widely believed that these companies have, in a sense, been co-opted by their employees; they do not express goals of short-term profitability but rather pay some cost in order to maintain stability of employment through difficult times. In a real sense, these work organizations may have created an alternative to village life.

THE IDEAL TYPES: A, J, and Z

In this section, we will describe three ideal types of work organization, in relation to certain environmental conditions in the society in which they operate. The three types are A, J, and Z. Type A represents the Western organization, especially the North American, Western European, and British forms. Type J represents the Japanese and mainland Chinese forms, and Type Z is an emer-

Type A (American)	Type J (Japanese)
Short-term employment	Lifetime employment
Individual decision-making	Consensual decision-making
Individual responsibility	Collective responsibility
Rapid evaluation and promotion	Slow evaluation and promotion
Explicit, formalized control	Implicit, informal control
Specialized career path	Nonspecialized career path
Segmented concern	Holistic concern

gent form which is particularly suited to the United States of America today. These ideal types are never to be found in their pure forms. They represent analytical variables and each system or ideal type has evolved in response to a particular set of environmental characteristics. Each type seems to be a valid representation of many present-day work organizations.

Length of employment. Length of employment refers to the average number of years served within the corporation, considering all employees. This is important in two respects: First, if the mean number of years of tenure is high, then employees will be more familiar with the workings of the organization and more likely to have developed friendships among their co-workers; second, if the new employee anticipates a long career within one organization, he or she will be willing to incur greater personal costs in order to become integrated into the culture of the organization.

Mode of decision-making. The mode of decision-making refers to the typical ways of dealing with nonroutine problems. In individual decision-making, the manager may solicit information or opinions from others or may not, but he or she expects and is expected by others to arrive at a decision without obligation to consider the views of others. Under consensual decision-making, the manager will not decide until others who will be affected have had sufficient time to offer their views so that they feel they have been fairly heard and are willing to support the decision even though they may not feel that it is the best one.

Responsibility. Responsibility is not easily distinguished from decision-making style in all cases, but it represents an important, independent dimension. Individual responsibility as a value is a necessary precondition to the conferring of rewards upon individuals in a meritocracy. It is possible that a manager could engage in consensual decision-making while clearly retaining individual responsibility for the decision. Indeed, we will argue that the Type Z organization exhibits just this combination. In the J organization, we observe that responsibility for overseeing projects and for accepting rewards or punishments is borne collectively and jointly by all members of a subunit.

American companies in Japan which have attempted to introduce the notion of individual responsibility among managers and among blue-collar workers have found strong resistance from their employees. Indeed, it is largely due to a collective view of responsibility that Japanese organizations have relatively little conflict between individuals and between organizational subunits. In the United States, however, individual responsibility is such a central part of the national culture that no organization can replace it with the collective value of the J type.

Evaluation and promotion. The speed with which evaluation and promotion of individuals take place is self-explanatory, but its effects are subtle. If promotion is rapid, managers at any given level of the organization will be less completely socialized into the organizational culture than if promotion is slow. It follows that if the organization has had a history of rapid promotion for many years, it will not have as unified an atmosphere as will an organization with slower rates of upward mobility.

In addition to the effects on the atmosphere of an organization, the speed of evaluation has significant effects upon the character of interpersonal relationships. In an achievement-oriented organization, evaluations of performance must be free of dimensions which are not related to achievement. Specifically, friendship and kinship must be explicitly prohibited as criteria of evaluation. The supervisor can never know whether his or her evaluation of a subordinate is tinged with personal likes or dislikes if there is any personal attachment. The only solution open to this evaluator is an impersonal relationship. If evaluations occur rapidly, for example once each six months, only the direct supervisor will be charged with the responsibility of rendering the evaluation, and he or she is thus blocked from forming personal, friendship ties with the subordinate.

If major evaluations occur only once every five or ten years, however (as is common in Japanese firms), then the evaluation is no longer explicitly rendered by one superior but rather emerges through a nonexplicit process of agreement between the many superiors who know the subordinate. Under this condition, the direct superior is freed from the need to preserve an "objective" attitude toward the subordinate and thus can take a personal interest in him or her. Under rapid evaluation, therefore, the formation of personal ties is much less likely to occur than under slow evaluation.

Control. The dimension of control is represented in the ideal type in an oversimplified manner. However, we can identify in Type A organizations the use of explicit standards, rules and regulations, and measures of performance as the primary technique of ensuring that actual performance meets desired performance. In the Type J, by contrast, expectations of behavior or of output are not explicitly stated but rather are to be deduced from a more general understanding of the corporate philosophy.

For example, in a visit to a Japanese bank in California, both the Japanese president and the American vice-presidents of the bank accused the other of being unable to formulate objectives. The Americans meant that the Japanese president could not or would not give them explicit, quantified targets to attain over the next three to six months, while the Japanese meant that the Americans could not see that once they understood the company's philosophy, they would be able to deduce for themselves the proper objective for any conceivable situation.

Career path. The degree to which a career path is specialized according to function or not differs greatly between organizational types. In the A organization, an upwardly mobile manager will remain within a functional specialty, going from bookkeeper to clerical supervisor to assistant department head of accounting to head of the accounting department, for example. In the J organization, the individual's career path is not specialized by function but may go from bookkeeper to supervisor of the planning department.

A specialized career path yields professionalization, decreases organizational loyalty, and facilitates movement of the individual from one firm to another. A nonspecialized career path yields localism, increases organizational loyalty, and impedes inter-firm mobility. Career specialization also increases problems of coordination between individuals and subunits, while nonspecialization eases the coordination problem. On the other hand, career specialization yields the scale economies of task specialization and expertise, whereas nonspecialized career paths sacrifice these benefits. Note that the A and J organizations may be the same in formal structure; they may have equal divisional separation, for example, but individuals will move through those subunits in quite different patterns.

Concern. Concern refers to the holism with which employees view each other and especially to the concern with which the superior views the subordinate. In the A organization, the supervisor regards the subordinate in a purely task-oriented manner and may consider it improper to inquire into the personal life of the subordinate. The manager of the J organization considers it part of his or her role to be fully informed of the personal circumstances of each subordinate, including the health of the subordinate and his or her family, their financial condition, and their nonwork-related aspirations. This concern may of course reflect interest in the value of the employee to the firm rather than a concern motivated by altruism.

Where Type A Thrives

The systemic nature of each type is best understood by putting each in an environmental context. The A type has developed in a society which is characterized by high rates of mobility of individuals, and which supports norms of independence, self-reliance, and individual responsibility. A work organization in such a setting must contend with high rates of inter-firm mobility and a short average tenure of employment. To the extent possible, an organization in this setting will reduce interdependence between individuals so as to avoid the start-up costs of replacing one part of a team. Individual decision-making and individual responsibility both provide an adaptive response to rapid change of personnel.

If inter-firm mobility is high, it is difficult to intergrate new employees completely into the "style" of the company. Thus a segmented concern will evolve because concern for the whole person presents an impossible problem to an organization with high turnover. As a result, however, the employee has only limited, contractual ties to the organization, has not internalized the values of the organization, and must be dealt with in a relationship in which control is explicit and formalized.

In addition, the organization has a relatively short time in which to realize productive benefits from the necessary investment in the individual (the costs of search and of whatever minimal training is necessary) and it can best realize these benefits by having that person follow a highly specialized career path in which learning occurs rapidly and scale economies are soon achieved. Finally, rapid turnover requires replacement of managers and thus rapid promotion of those at lower levels. Promotion must be preceded by evaluation at least to preserve the impression, if not the fact, of a meritocracy, and thus evaluation also will occur rapidly.

How Type J Evolves

Type J organizations have evolved in a society in which individual mobility has historically been low and which supported norms of collectivism. Traditional feudal loyalties in Japan have been transferred to major industrial institutions, with both owners and employees taking the appropriate historical roles of lord and vassal. Under this condition, employment in those major firms is generally for a lifetime. If employees are expected to be in the same firm for a lifetime, then control can be implicit and internalized rather than explicit and formalized (as in the A type). These employees need not follow specialized career paths, because the organization can invest in them for a long period of time and be assured of repayment in later years.

Thus they follow nonspecialized career paths, which has the effect of making them experts in the organization rather than experts in some function. They are no longer interchangeable with other organizations, since their particular set of skills and values is unique to one firm. But that is not a cost to them or to the firm: Rather, their loyalty to the firm has increased and the firm need not closely monitor them, thus saving managerial overhead. Furthermore, problems of coordination are greatly reduced, since employees have both the information and the inclination to enable them to accommodate each other in jointly taking action.

Since these individuals are to spend a lifetime together, they have an interest in maintaining harmonious relationships and thus to engage in consensual decision-making. The larger culture strongly supports norms of collectivism which are mirrored in the organization. No individual can properly take credit or blame for actions, since organizational action by its very nature is a joint product of many individuals. Since turnover and thus promotion occurs slowly, evaluation need not proceed quickly, so that many observations of the individual by several people are accumulated over a period of years before the first major evaluation is made. By taking the pressure off of a single superior for the evaluation, this then frees him or her to take a holistic concern in the employee.

Since each of the ideal types represents a natural adaptation to a particular environment, we must now explain how the J type has apparently succeeded in the United States which provided the social environment in which the A type evolved.

In order to answer this question, we have spent the past 14 months interviewing managers from a large number of companies. In particular, the interviews focused on those American companies which, by reputation, have many of the characteristics of the Type J. Out of these interviews has come a conception of a third ideal type which initially appeared to be the J, but differs from it in some essential characteristics.

Type Z (Modified American)

Long-term employment
Consensual decision-making
Individual responsibility
Slow evaluation and promotion
Implicit, informal control with explicit, formalized measures
Moderately specialized career path
Holistic concern, including family

The ideal Type Z combines a basic cultural commitment to individualistic values with a highly collective, nonindividual pattern of interaction. It simultaneously satisfies old norms of independence and present needs for affiliation. Employment is effective for a lifetime although not officially so, and turnover is low. Decision-making is consensual and in these companies there is often a highly self-conscious attempt to preserve the consensual mode. However, it is still the individual who is ultimately the decision-maker and responsibility remains individual. This procedure clearly puts strains on the individual, who is held responsible for decisions singly but must arrive at them collectively. These strains are mitigated by the fact that evaluation and promotion take place slowly and that the basic control is implicit and subtle. Thus the complexities of collective decision-making are taken into account in rendering personal evaluations, but there will still be explicit measures of performance as in the Type A.

Promotion and Punishment Slow

It is common to hear it said in the Z organization that although there are lots of formal accounting measures of performance, the real evaluation is subjective and highly personal. No one gets rapidly promoted or punished in a Z organization solely because his or her performance scores are good or bad. In an A organization, by contrast, people's careers often succeed or fail solely on the explicit performance measures, as must be the case in any purely formalized system. Career paths tend to be moderately specialized, but are quite nonspecialized by comparison with the Type A organization. Again, the slowness of evaluation and the stability of membership promote a holistic concern for people, particularly from superior to subordinate.

In the Z organization, this holism includes the employee and his or her family in an active manner. This is necessary because if the organization were to include the employee but exclude the family, as in Japan, the family would be completely abandoned. In Japan, wives and children have their own stable social groups which provide order in their lives, and they can adjust to the absence of the husband and father. In the United States, where wives and children move frequently (or if they don't, their friends do), such supportive groups do not exist for them. Traditionally, the A organization has responded by including only a segment of the husband, in a sense leaving the rest of him for his family. The Z organization, by contrast, includes the husband and his family in the organization. That means that family members regularly interact with other organization members and their families and feel an identification with the organization.

It is evident that the ideal Type Z combines characteristics of both the A and J types in a unique pattern, but what is the meaning of this ideal type? More directly, why is the Z a useful type in thinking about American organizations if the A type is the natural adaptation to this society? If the ideal type represents a natural adaptation to a culture, but a second ideal type can be accommodated, the social conditions must have changed.

In this case, the critical aspect of the environment is its ability to provide stable affiliations for individuals. It has been argued above that the traditional sources of affiliation in the American society have been the family, the church, the neighborhood, the voluntary association, and the long-term friendship. It was under these conditions that Type A organizations evolved. It has further been argued that urbanization and geographical mobility have weakened these sources of affiliation.

But the values which supported those patterns will change more slowly. Those values support the notion of partial inclusion, of individuality, of the Type A organization. Thus, we find ourselves largely in a society unable to provide affiliation, and with work organizations not organized to do so. Clearly, if we are to return to a balanced state, it will be a new one in which affiliation comes mostly from the organization and not from the society at large.

Not all people need the same level of affiliation (or, for that matter, of achievement or of power). However, Abraham Maslow asserts that all people have a need for affiliation, belongingness, or love, and that this need can be satisfied through the feeling that they are part of a group or company.* If we accept this thesis, people who have low affiliation in the society and in (or with) the workplace will have unfulfilled needs for affiliation; they will experience "anomie," the sensation that there are no anchors in life, no standards, and thus a feeling of being lost.

If, it is true that American society in general is moving towards a low affiliation state, if it is true that neither the church, the family, the neighborhood, the club, nor the childhood friendship is likely to make a comeback, then it falls to the work organization to provide the glue which will hold this society together. No other institution plays as central a role in the lives of Americans as does their place of work. No other institution has the same opportunity to restore the spirit of community and of belongingness which is essential to any society.

---

*Abraham Maslow is the originator of the thesis that people have a "need hierarchy," ranging from "physical" needs, through "security, social," and "ego" needs, to the highest level of need, "self-actualization." An individual's place on this hierarchy can vary with the person *and* the society.

That is not to suggest that the work organization will in any way replace or compete with our other national institutions. Quite the opposite: If the company provides a strong basic stability in people's lives, then the family, the church, the neighborhood can all flourish.

Type Z Could Save a Marriage

Consider also the possible effect on marriage. It is often said that a primary reason for the soaring rate of divorce in the United States is that the institution of marriage is now expected to carry, single handed, a burden that formerly was shared by many sources of support. Throughout the history of the monogamous relationship, it has always been true that each man had a stable group of other men with whom he spent much of his time and with whom he could share many of his deepest personal concerns. Likewise, each woman had a stable female society to help her to carry life's burdens.

It is only in the last few decades that a husband has been expected to single-handedly carry all of his wife's burdens and she to shoulder his. That is simply too large a load. If each is involved in a Type Z organization, however, then the possibility of meaningful contact with other adults exists, and a good deal of the pressure is taken off the husband-wife relationship. What a relief it is to have worked out one's frustrations and disappointments with sympathetic colleagues at work and return home in the evening ready to participate in more pleasant pursuits than the taking out of those anxieties and tensions!

Until recently, the Type A organization was the most successful form in our society. When people had relatives, neighbors, and churches, they didn't need Dr. Spock to tell them why the baby was purple and they didn't need a company that provided them with a rich network of social contacts. In a few cases, however, companies grew up in small towns, or in places like California that were populated by immigrants, or in industries which required frequent relocation of employees.

In each instance, one side-effect was that people had no form of social contact available to them except through their employer. An extreme case is the military base, which seems to look, feel, and smell the same whether it is in Hawaii, Illinois, or New York. In order to make life possible under conditions of high mobility, the military had to develop a culture which would be familiar and secure no matter where its employees went.

In a sense, these organizations, both public and private, had created a social vacuum for their employees and then had to develop internal sources of support to replace what had been taken away. Now, the rest of the country is catching up with them as stable sources of support disappear everywhere. We can look to such models for ideas to show us how to cope with our new society.

For the professional manager, this suggests a new role, one which will be difficult for many to accept: the role of social intermediary. Managers are familiar with the concept of the financial intermediary, one who performs a service by bringing together providers of capital with users of capital. In a like manner, every manager will have to bring together people who are simultaneously givers of support and needers of support.

The company which successfully builds such a culture will be the company which attracts and holds talented employees; it will have a valuable stock of good will among its employees. In short, it will provide a commodity that is scarce and highly valued among members of our labor force at all levels of education and income. The professional manager will no longer be able to say to himself or herself that the only thing that matters is performance or that what employees do outside the office is purely their affair. Without invading their right to privacy, he or she will have to clearly take an interest in "whole persons" and will have to believe that his or her obligations to them are broad and ambiguous rather than limited and contractual.

At this point, some will object that they personally will never support a Type Z approach in their company or that it would never work in their industry. Many of them are right. We have already pointed out that our society contains a range of people; some will always prefer an employer who leaves them alone, who evaluates them purely on objective measures, who recognizes achievement through rapid promotion even over the heads of others. Of course, there will always be organizations for such people and for such tastes, but the trend will be towards Type Z.

Type Z Not for Everyone

In some industries, however, stability of employment is not currently possible; aerospace is one good example. In such an industry, a Type Z organization would be harmful; people would build rich ties with each other and a control system based on personal knowledge. Both would be wrenched and destroyed when the contract comes to an end and massive layoffs become necessary. Clearly, the Type Z form will not be for everyone.

Finally, a word on what this all implies for the graduate schools of business and for their recent MBA graduates. It is notable that many of the Type Z companies hire few if any MBAs. Those which do hire MBAs in large numbers go to great lengths to teach them the company's way of doing things, which amounts to teaching them the local culture. Why this difficulty of integrating MBAs into Type Z companies?

The Type Z form rests on subtlety, on knowing the local customs, on implicit rather than explicit decision rules. No one can successfully operate in a Type Z without having been thoroughly acculturated. Most business schools, in contrast, teach their students to be explicit about everything—how they organize, who reports to whom, how plans are made, what the goals and objectives are, what decision rules are used.

The whole approach is inimical to the delicacy of a Type Z organization. Thus the choice faced by the Type Z is: either avoid MBAs and thus avoid indigestion, or hire MBAs for their talent and their skills but invest heavily in acculturating them and then hope that they don't leave. If the Type Z naively hires a flock of MBAs and throws them in without carefully preparing them, disaster will result, as many companies have discovered, much to their regret.

From the point of view of the young MBA, there is an equally perplexing but less tractable problem. If the MBA takes a job in a Type Z, then rapid promotion is virtually impossible, disillusionment quickly sets in, and an exit follows shortly. If the MBA goes instead to a Type A company, then rapid promotion is possible; but the other MBAs are being promoted at an equally rapid rate and, since motion is relative, he or she is standing still.

This occurs because the Type A company is designed to deal with high turnover, and thus most of the opportunity for control and for leadership is built into the structure of the company so that departures are not so disruptive. Because the structure contains most of the power, the young manager has little opportunity to take the bull by the horns, have a great deal of discretion, and show what he or she can do. There is no discretion to be had, no bull to be taken by the horns. Thus, the disillusioned young manager leaves to find a company that has really rapid promotion possibilities, finds even less available authority, and is caught in a trap.

How the dilemma of the ambitious MBA is to be resolved remains a puzzle. To return to our central point, however, the future problem of the professional manager seems relatively clear. Our society, which has been in a constant process of change during its turbulent 200 years, has reached a critical point.

People no longer donate blood in sufficient quantities to meet society's needs and so hospitals must buy it from indigents; violent crimes increasingly involve a victim who is completely unknown to the assailant; workers feel less and less commitment to their employers; all of us long for stability and for structure in our lives.

These changes all signify a decline in belongingness. They suggest the fate assigned by Homans to those societies which lose the feeling of membership: We will become ". . . a dust heap of individuals without links to one another."